Inspiration
Promise Book

INSPIRATION PROMISE BOOK

by David and Barbara Cerullo

ISBN: 978-1-887600-94-1

Published by

INSPIRATION
MINISTRIES

INSPIRATION MINISTRIES
PO BOX 7750
CHARLOTTE, NC 28241
+1 803-578-1899

inspiration.org

Printed in the United States of America.

DEDICATION

In grateful appreciation to our faithful Inspiration Partners...

Your prayers and financial seeds have accomplished great things for God's Kingdom, both in this life and in eternity.

Your reward in Heaven will be great!

Inspiration Promise Book

TABLE *of* CONTENTS

GOD'S PROMISES FOR PRAYING HIS WORD

GOD'S PROMISES FOR WHEN YOU NEED...

GOD'S PROMISES FOR WHEN YOU FEEL...

GOD'S PROMISES FOR WHEN YOU NEED REASSURANCE ABOUT...

GOD'S PROMISES FOR WHEN YOU'RE STRUGGLING WITH...

GOD'S PROMISES FOR WHAT TO DO WHEN YOU'RE...

INTRODUCTION

by
David and Barbara Cerullo

HELLO, PRECIOUS FRIENDS.
As we write this introduction to the *Inspiration Promise Book*, the sun is shining brightly and the flowers and lawns are desperately thirsty for cool drinks of water.

Do you ever feel like this in your relationship with the Lord? Thirsty for more of Him and eager to drink deeply from His Word? We do.

The psalmist describes this feeling in Psalm 42:1-2: *"As the deer pants for the water brooks, so pants my soul for You, O God. My soul thirsts for God, for the living God. When shall I come and appear before God?"*

In John 7:37-38, Jesus reveals that He's the source of living water for all who are thirsty: *"If anyone thirsts, let him come to Me and drink. He who believes in Me, as the Scripture has said, out of his heart will flow rivers of living water."*

And in Isaiah 55:1, there is a wonderful invitation from the Lord to us, His children: *"Ho! Everyone who thirsts, come to the waters."* Before we can pray with power and authority, we must first come to God in quiet times of rest, prayer, and worship to drink deeply of Him. Then we will be able to effectively intercede for whatever concerns are on our hearts: our precious children and grandchildren, our health, our emotions, our finances, our emotions…or whatever other situation needs God's intervention.

We've prepared the *Inspiration Promise Book* as a powerful tool to help you spend time with Jesus, learning His ways and drinking the living water He offers you.

We encourage you today, no matter how busy you are…no matter how tired…no matter how painful and upsetting your circumstances may be, go to Him and drink deeply from His Word. Let His Holy Spirit refresh and restore your weary soul.

When you do, God's Word promises that out of your life will flow rivers of living water—pouring out on your loved ones and a needy world. As God promised Abraham, He is saying to you today: *"I will bless you…and you shall be a blessing"* (Genesis 12:2).

Love in Christ,

David & Barbara

GOD'S PROMISES
for
PRAYING HIS WORD

THE POWER OF PRAYING GOD'S WORD

IN FACING the challenging circumstances of everyday living, the Bible is your lifeline and a vital tool for energizing your prayer life.

God makes a precious promise about the power and effectiveness of praying His Word: *"So shall My Word be that goes forth from My mouth; it shall **not** return to Me void, but it **shall** accomplish what I please, and it **shall** prosper in the thing for which I sent it"* (Isaiah 55:11).

This is so encouraging. God assures us that when we pray His Word and declare it as true in our life, He will do what we're asking Him to do.

The Bible tells us, *"Death and life are in the power of the tongue…"* (Proverbs 18:21). There's a powerful impact whenever we align our words with the truth of Scripture!

When we pray God's Word, we're calling upon the Lord to honor His promises to breathe *life* into our circumstances and send blessings to our loved ones.

These Promises Are for You

God's Word is *full* of promises, and the *Inspiration Promise Book* you are holding is just a taste of the great things the Lord has ordained for your life.

But perhaps you have a lingering doubt when you read the promises in God's Word. "How do I know these promises are really meant for *me*?" you may wonder.

The apostle Paul seems to anticipate this question when he writes: *"Whatever things were written before were written for our learning, that we through the patience and comfort of the Scriptures might have hope"* (Romans 15:4). The truths of Scripture were written with *us* in mind!

Paul says this again in 2 Corinthians 1:18-20:

> *As God is faithful, our word to you was not Yes and No. For the Son of God, Jesus Christ, who was preached among you by us—by me, Silvanus, and Timothy—was not Yes and No, but in Him was Yes. For all the promises of God in Him are Yes, and in Him Amen, to the glory of God through us.*

In Christ, ALL of God's promises are "YES" to *you*!

PRAYING FOR YOUR CHILDREN AND GRANDCHILDREN

IN PAUL'S SECOND LETTER to his spiritual son Timothy, we learn that it was the powerful faith of Timothy's mother and grandmother that helped prepare this young man for tremendous ministry (2 Timothy 1:5). So don't underestimate the impact *your* faith can have on *your* children and grandchildren!

Children and grandchildren can be one of our greatest sources of joy. And because we love them so much, we also may suffer greatly on their account.

It's especially difficult when our children choose to turn their backs on the Lord and walk away from what they know to be true and good and right. As parents or grandparents, we may experience intense pain from their poor choices, and sometimes our hearts may break with grief.

There will be times when we'll walk through painful, grief-filled seasons with our children—seasons when all we can do is cry out to God on their behalf. Thankfully, we can trust the Lord to draw our children to walk closely with Him and serve Him with their whole hearts. Yet there may be valleys we have to walk through before we see God answer our prayers and intervene in our children's lives.

Claiming the Word

During difficult times with your children, there are important principles to remember as you pray God's Word over your kids or grandkids. It's really so simple!

First, ask the Lord to lead you to Scriptures to pray over the specific situations of your children or grandchildren. Then in your quiet time, during a Sunday message, in a conversation with a close friend, or in some other way, the Holy Spirit will give you verses that you can turn into powerful prayers.

For example, one time when we were praying passionately for our son Ben, the Lord led us to Jeremiah 31:16-17:

> *"Refrain your voice from weeping, and your eyes from tears; for your work shall be rewarded," says the* LORD, *"and they shall come back from the land of the enemy."*

> *"There is hope in your future," says the* LORD, *"that your children shall come back to their own border."*

When we read these words, we cried for joy. We had spent so many hours interceding on Ben's behalf, weeping and broken over his situation. God used His Word to remind us that He had a specific plan for Ben, and we made these verses a prayer for our son by inserting his name:

> "Thank You, God, that our prayers will be rewarded and that Ben WILL return from the land of the enemy. Thank You that there is hope. In Jesus' name, we declare today that Ben WILL come again to the borders of our home and God's Kingdom!"

And soon after this, Ben returned to the Lord! As we aligned our prayers with specific promises from God's Word, the Holy Spirit moved powerfully on Ben's heart.

More Scriptures to Claim

There are many other great Scriptures you can use as prayers over your children or grandchildren:

"Yes, I have loved [name] *with an everlasting love; therefore with lovingkindness I have drawn* [name]. *Again I will rebuild* [name], *and* [name] *shall be rebuilt"* (Jeremiah 31:3-4).

"But now, thus says the Lord, *who created* [name], *and who formed* [name]: *'Fear not, for I have redeemed* [name]; *I have called* [name] *by name;* [he/she] *is Mine. When* [name] *passes through the waters, I will be with* [him/her]; *and through the rivers, they shall not overflow* [him/her]. *When* [name] *walks through the fire,* [he/she] *shall not be burned, nor shall the flame scorch* [him/her]'"* (Isaiah 43:1-2).

"[Name] *is poor and needy; make haste to help* [him/her], *O God! You are [name's] help and* [his/her] *deliverer; O* Lord, *do not delay"* (Psalm 70:5).

These verses are just a sample! Ask the Lord to lead you to other specific Scriptures that He wants you to use as powerful prayers of intercession over your children and grandchildren.

Our Prayer for Your Children and Grandchildren

Be encouraged today to pray and believe God's Word over your generations. Pray, watch, and wait for the Lord to bring about His destiny for their lives, and you will not be disappointed.

And now we would like to pray an adaptation of Isaiah 44:2-4 over you, your children, and your grandchildren:

"Thus says the Lord who made you and your children and grandchildren, and who formed you from the womb, who will help you: Fear not, my precious friend, for God has chosen you. He will pour water on you who are thirsty, and floods on the dry ground; He will pour His Spirit on your descendants, and His blessing on your offspring: they will spring up among the grass like willows by the watercourses. In Jesus' name. AMEN."

*N*EVER GIVE UP!

THE BIBLE TEACHES that perseverance is one of the most important ingredients for answered prayer. According to Hebrews 6:12, we inherit God's promises through *"faith and patience"*— not faith alone!

In Luke 18:1-8, Jesus says we *"always ought to pray and not lose heart."* He goes on to tell the story of a woman who wouldn't stop pounding on the judge's door until she got a response, and that's exactly the posture we took when our children Ben and Becky seemed to be straying from God. We continually pounded on Heaven's door until we saw the fruit from our prayers manifested in their lives. We prayed and we prayed, and then we prayed some more.

Jesus promises us:

> *So I say to you, ask, and it will be given to you; seek, and you will find; knock, and it will be opened to you. For everyone who asks receives, and he who seeks, finds, and to him who knocks, it will be opened* (Luke 11:9-10).

The literal Greek translation of this passage says, *"Ask and **keep on** asking...seek and **keep on** seeking...knock and **keep on** knocking."* We must pray and keep on praying! We must never give up!

Praying with Confidence

This is true whenever we're seeking God's intervention in a troubling situation in our lives. Whether we are in need of a physical healing, a financial breakthrough, a new job, or a restored relationship, we must cry out to God with faith and tenacity.

Scripture tells us that Satan is like a restless, starving, roaring lion, pacing about and searching for victims to devour (1 Peter 5:8-9). He never stops prowling, so we must never stop praying. Our prayers are our greatest weapon as we wage war on behalf of our own destiny or our loved ones. And one of our most powerful prayer weapons is our ability to pray God's Word.

This truth is so encouraging! What a joy to have confidence that when we pray the Word, God will do whatever we're asking Him to do.

Let's be honest. When our circumstances are desperate, it's easy to cling to our own opinions about what God should do. Yet God's ways are not our ways (Isaiah 55:8-9), so we don't always *know* what is best in a certain situation. Only He knows what must happen for peoples' hearts to change. This is why it's so important for us to pray Scriptures over our lives and loved ones.

Let Go!

When we experience difficult and painful times, there may be days when we struggle with doubt. But the Lord continuously reminds us that we are *His*. He loves us so much and is always carving out great testimonies from our experiences and challenges.

God asks us to trust Him with everything we hold dear, and sometimes He wants us to "back off" so He can move in our hearts and lives. We must choose to "let go" and place everything in His loving hands.

We encourage you to pray and totally surrender *every* concern to God. Ask Him to do whatever is needed to bring about His Kingdom in your situation.

Even when things seem to get worse before they get better, never forget that God and His mercies are new every morning (Lamentations 3:21-23). He loves you—and your loved ones—more than you can comprehend. You can trust Him 100% with your future...and theirs.

Never give up on the Lord as you ask Him to transform the difficult situations in your life. He is already at work, and He has a wonderful plan to bless you and your loved ones.

Ask and keep on asking...seeking...knocking...praying. Keep believing, keep trusting, and you *WILL* see God's goodness and faithfulness in your life and the lives of your loved ones.

This Scripture is our prayer for *you* today:

> *Wait on the* LORD *and be of good courage, and He shall strengthen your heart; wait, I say, on the* LORD (Psalm 27:14)!

Remember: Never give up on God, for He will never give up on you (Philippians 1:6).

MEDITATE ON THESE THINGS

SOMETIMES WHEN WE PRAY, we may be expecting God to miraculously touch us and give us some kind of instant revelation. But God rarely taps us on the shoulder with an immediate impartation of knowledge, wisdom, or understanding. Learning one of His lessons usually takes time, study, and prayer.

Please don't be offended by this, but too many Christians are like little birds in a nest, waiting impatiently for their mother to bring them food. Their little mouths are open, and they're chirping, "Hurry, hurry, we're hungry!"

Of course, little birds are helpless and can't do anything to help themselves, but are we? As Believers, we can't just passively wait to be fed Scriptural truths by teachers and preachers. We must learn to feed ourselves from God's Word.

While we believe so strongly in the power of prayer, it's just as important to set aside focused times for studying God's Word. If you truly desire to grow in your relationship with the Lord and become more like Him, you *must* do this.

Applying God's Truths to Your Life

Many of us have access to a smorgasbord of Christian conventions, Bible studies, church services, and TV preachers. These opportunities can be a real blessing, and many lives are changed because of them. If we wanted to, we could just go from one banqueting table to another, because God's Word is available in so many places in our country.

But if we aren't careful, we can become too dependent on this spoon-feeding. It's possible to become so spiritually "fat" that we're useless for anything productive in God's Kingdom.

Just hearing a message and agreeing with it doesn't mean we actually *learned* it. We can admire what was said and even accept God's truth, but until we *act* upon it, we haven't allowed His truth to become a reality in our lives. We need to stop, meditate on what we've heard, and begin applying it to our lives before moving on to the next lesson God has in store for us.

Most Believers don't practice Scripture meditation, and so they lose much of the benefit they could be gaining from what they read in the Bible or hear preached. The Parable of the Sower in Matthew 13:19 describes this condition: *"When anyone hears the message about the kingdom and does not understand it, the evil one comes and snatches away what was sown in his heart."*

This story is Jesus' explanation of God's Word being sown into our hearts. He describes different types of soil to represent our various human reactions to God's truth. According to this verse, when Scripture doesn't become an integral part of our life, the enemy comes and immediately steals it from us. His goal is to rob us of the most important source of our spiritual growth: God's Word.

The Special Role of Meditation

Keep in mind that transcendental meditation (an Eastern religious practice) is very different from Biblical meditation. While transcendental meditation is a humanistic mental process involving chanting and incantation, Biblical meditation focuses solely on the Lord and His Word.

This really shouldn't be so controversial, since Scripture clearly *tells us* to meditate:

> *This Book of the Law shall not depart from your mouth, but you shall **meditate** in it day and night, that you may observe to **do** according to all that is written in it. For then you will make your way prosperous, and then you will have good success* (Joshua 1:8).

> ***Meditate** on these things; give yourself entirely to them, that your progress may be evident to all* (1 Timothy 4:15).

> ***Meditate** within your heart on your bed, and be still* (Psalm 4:4).

> *Finally, brethren, whatever things are true, whatever things are noble, whatever things are just, whatever things are pure, whatever things are lovely, whatever things are of good report, if there is any virtue and if there is anything praiseworthy—**meditate** on these things* (Philippians 4:8).

In all of these verses, we are instructed and encouraged to use our *minds* to apply the truths of God's Word to our lives. We are told to meditate on the Lord, His Word, and the things of His Kingdom.

A Common Biblical Practice

Meditation is a spiritual discipline very familiar to the Biblical writers:

His delight is in the law of the LORD, and in His law he meditates day and night (Psalm 1:2).

When I remember You on my bed, I meditate on You in the night watches (Psalm 63:6).

I will also meditate on all Your work, and talk of Your deeds (Psalm 77:12).

I will meditate on Your precepts, and contemplate Your ways (Psalm 119:15).

Your servant meditates on Your statutes (Psalm 119:23).

My eyes are awake through the night watches, that I may meditate on Your word (Psalm 119:148).

I meditate on all Your works; I muse on the work of Your hands (Psalm 143:5).

I will meditate on the glorious splendor of Your majesty, and on Your wondrous works (Psalm 145:5).

A book of remembrance was written before Him for those who fear the LORD and who meditate on His name (Malachi 3:16).

With so many references in the Bible to meditation, isn't it amazing we don't hear more about it in the church today? Yet this is an important tool as we pursue greater intimacy with the Lord and greater application of His Word in our lives.

Setting Aside Special Time

When we devote extended time to meditation, it can be wonderful!

Some meditation time can be focused on prayer, but some of it can be spent just reflecting on the many questions you want to ask God. Taking the time to think these through and look up what the Bible has to say about them can cause meditation to feel like a luxury, and it will create an even greater hunger for you to spend time doing this in the future.

Although it may not be easy to find time for meditation, this is worth the fight for you to keep growing in your relationship with the Lord.

I so enjoy meditating on God's Word and searching for His answers to the questions on my heart. It's a wonderful chance for me to be my true self and experience peace and safety in His presence. I always come away relaxed and refreshed from this special time of communion with Him.

Finding a Special Place

Just as we need to set aside special times for prayer and meditation, it also helps to have a special place where we can get away for undistracted fellowship with the Lord. This is beautifully portrayed in a short story by David Wolfe entitled, "Teaching Your Children About God":

There was a rabbi who had a son. It was soon noticed by the man that the young boy was often in the forest near their house. The boy's father had become worried since he wasn't sure of the dangers his son might face.

He decided to speak to the boy about this, and asked him why he was spending so much time alone in the forest. The boy replied that he was going there to find God.

The rabbi, happy to hear that his son was in search of the Divine, noted that the boy didn't have to go into the woods to find God, "Because," he added, "God is the same everywhere."

The boy's answer?

"Yes, Dad, but I am not."

It's easy to identify with the boy. Some people may not understand why you love to get away with your Bible and be alone as you meditate on God's Word...but that's okay. Alone time with Him provides a fantastic opportunity for you to truly be "you."

God can be so real to you when you're alone with Him. You can cry or laugh, and you don't have to explain yourself to anyone! You can clear away all the cobwebs from your heart and mind, and then truly experience and hear from the Lord as you meditate on His Word.

We receive many requests from our Inspiration Partners who want us to pray they will grow closer to the Lord...and *we do.* However, we always want them to understand that they must be dedicated and disciplined in setting aside their *own* time to study and meditate on God's Word.

Know this: Absolutely none of the time you spend with the Lord and His Word will be wasted. You *always* will come away renewed and refreshed!

We pray this *Inspiration Promise Book* will help you draw closer to God as you devote yourself to finding a regular time and place to meet with Him.

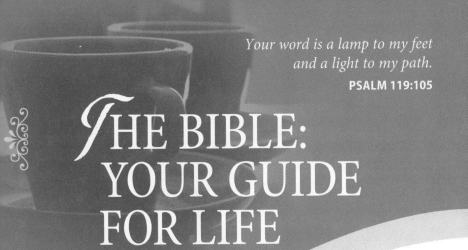

Your word is a lamp to my feet and a light to my path.

PSALM 119:105

THE BIBLE: YOUR GUIDE FOR LIFE

HAVE YOU EVER BEEN on a road trip to a strange city… without a map or a GPS unit? If so, you know what it feels like to lose your sense of direction.

Thankfully, God has given us a wonderful roadmap for our lives: the Bible. Its wisdom covers every situation and area of life, and we can be confident that its advice is *reliable*, because it is God's Word to us!

We created the *Inspiration Promise Book* to help you quickly find God's wisdom on the issues that affect your life. God describes His Word as nutritious spiritual food that will help you grow stronger in your relationship with Him: *"Desire the pure milk of the word, that you may grow thereby"* (1 Peter 2:2).

Forever, O Lord, Your word is settled in heaven.
Psalm 119:89

The commandment is a lamp, and the law a light; reproofs of instruction are the way of life.
Proverbs 6:23

Your testimonies also are my delight and my counselors.
Psalm 119:24

Man shall not live by bread alone; but man lives by every word that proceeds from the mouth of the Lord.
Deuteronomy 8:3

How can a young man cleanse his way? By taking heed according to Your word.
Psalm 119:9

The law of the Lord is perfect, converting the soul;
The testimony of the Lord is sure, making wise the simple;
The statutes of the Lord are right, rejoicing the heart;
The commandment of the Lord is pure, enlightening the eyes;
The fear of the Lord is clean, enduring forever;
The judgments of the Lord are true and righteous altogether.
More to be desired are they than gold,
Yea, than much fine gold;
Sweeter also than honey and the honeycomb.
Moreover by them Your servant is warned,
And in keeping them there is great reward.
Psalm 19:7-11

Your word I have hidden in my heart, that I might not sin against You.

PSALM 119:11

Jesus said to those Jews who believed Him, "If you abide in My word, you are My disciples indeed. And you shall know the truth, and the truth shall make you free."

JOHN 8:31-32

No prophecy of Scripture is of any private interpretation, for prophecy never came by the will of man, but holy men of God spoke as they were moved by the Holy Spirit.

2 PETER 1:20-21

This Book of the Law shall not depart from your mouth, but you shall meditate in it day and night, that you may observe to do according to all that is written in it. For then you will make your way prosperous, and then you will have good success.

JOSHUA 1:8

All Scripture is given by inspiration of God, and is profitable for doctrine, for reproof, for correction, for instruction in righteousness, that the man of God may be complete, thoroughly equipped for every good work.

2 TIMOTHY 3:16-17

PRAYER

HEAVENLY FATHER, *I want to know You better. Teach me Your Word. Reveal Your truth. Show me more about who You are and who I am in You.*

Thank You for giving me the Bible as my roadmap for life. May Your Word and Your Spirit guide me into the abundant life You've planned for me!

In Jesus' name. **AMEN.**

GOD WANTS TO ANSWER YOUR PRAYERS

GOD IS YOUR HEAVENLY FATHER. Like any good father, He wants to bless you and meet your needs.

After Jesus described how an earthly father wants to give good gifts to his children, He added, *"How much more will your Father who is in heaven give good things to those who ask Him!"* (Matthew 7:9-11).

Instead of being fearful or timid when we approach God in prayer, the Bible says, *"Let us therefore come boldly to the throne of grace, that we may obtain mercy and find grace to help in time of need"* (Hebrews 4:16).

Whatever your need is today, you can boldly approach your Heavenly Father to intervene in your situation!

Ask, and it will be given to you; seek, and you will find; knock, and it will be opened to you. For everyone who asks receives, and he who seeks finds, and to him who knocks it will be opened. Or what man is there among you who, if his son asks for bread, will give him a stone? Or if he asks for a fish, will he give him a serpent? If you then, being evil, know how to give good gifts to your children, how much more will your Father who is in heaven give good things to those who ask Him!

MATTHEW 7:7-11

Delight yourself also in the LORD, and He shall give you the desires of your heart.

PSALM 37:4

You do not have because you do not ask.

JAMES 4:2

The LORD is near to all who call upon Him, to all who call upon Him in truth. He will fulfill the desire of those who fear Him; He also will hear their cry and save them.

PSALM 145:18-19

This is the confidence that we have in Him, that if we ask anything according to His will, He hears us. And if we know that He hears us, whatever we ask, we know that we have the petitions that we have asked of Him.

1 JOHN 5:14-15

GOD WANTS TO ANSWER YOUR PRAYERS

Men always ought to pray and not lose heart.

LUKE 18:1

Whatever things you ask in prayer, believing, you will receive.

MATTHEW 21:22

If two of you agree on earth concerning anything that they ask, it will be done for them by My Father in heaven.

MATTHEW 18:19

Whatever you ask in My name, that I will do, that the Father may be glorified in the Son.

JOHN 14:13

If you abide in Me, and My words abide in you, you will ask what you desire, and it shall be done for you.

JOHN 15:7

Call to Me, and I will answer you, and show you great and mighty things, which you do not know.

JEREMIAH 33:3

Whatever we ask we receive from Him, because we keep His commandments and do those things that are pleasing in His sight.

1 JOHN 3:22

With God all things are possible.

MARK 10:27

PRAYER

HEAVENLY FATHER, *thank You for all the wonderful promises in Your Word! Thank You for being faithful to meet the needs of Your children when they cry out to You in faith.*

Teach me more of Your Word, and draw me into a more intimate relationship with You. Help me hear the voice of Your Holy Spirit more distinctly when I pray. Let me have the patience and persistence I need to wait upon You for the breakthroughs I seek.

In Jesus' name. **AMEN.**

GOD'S PROMISES
for
WHEN YOU NEED...

CONFIDENCE

FEELINGS OF FEAR and inadequacy can steal our confidence, boldness, and peace of mind. Such feelings attempt to paralyze us from stepping into God's highest will for our lives.

But in the midst of all the challenges of life, God wants us to put our trust in Him. When we do, He gives us the confidence we need to find victory in every situation. This confidence doesn't come from a reliance on our own ability, for the Bible says, *"we should not trust in ourselves but in God"* (2 Corinthians 1:9).

Do you want this kind of unshakable confidence in your life? Then remember the words of the apostle Paul: *"Not that we are sufficient of ourselves to think of anything as being from ourselves, but our sufficiency is from God"* (2 Corinthians 3:5).

We may boldly say: "The Lord is my helper; I will not fear. What can man do to me?"

HEBREWS 13:6

Do not cast away your confidence, which has great reward. For you have need of endurance, so that after you have done the will of God, you may receive the promise.

HEBREWS 10:35-36

Being confident of this very thing, that He who has begun a good work in you will complete it until the day of Jesus Christ.

PHILIPPIANS 1:6

The wicked flee when no one pursues, but the righteous are bold as a lion.

PROVERBS 28:1

The LORD God is my strength; He will make my feet like deer's feet, and He will make me walk on my high hills.

HABAKKUK 3:19

In all these things we are more than conquerors through Him who loved us.

ROMANS 8:37

This is the confidence that we have in Him, that if we ask anything according to His will, He hears us. And if we know that He hears us, whatever we ask, we know that we have the petitions that we have asked of Him.

1 JOHN 5:14-15

I am not ashamed of the gospel of Christ, for it is the power of God to salvation for everyone who believes, for the Jew first and also for the Greek. For in it the righteousness of God is revealed from faith to faith; as it is written, "The just shall live by faith."

ROMANS 1:16-17

"Not by might nor by power, but by My Spirit," says the LORD of hosts.

ZECHARIAH 4:6

The LORD will be your confidence, and will keep your foot from being caught.

PROVERBS 3:26

I can do all things through Christ who strengthens me.

PHILIPPIANS 4:13

Be strong and of good courage, do not fear nor be afraid of them; for the LORD your God, He is the One who goes with you. He will not leave you nor forsake you.

DEUTERONOMY 31:6

In the day when I cried out, You answered me, and made me bold with strength in my soul.

PSALM 138:3

Most assuredly, I say to you, he who believes in Me, the works that I do he will do also; and greater works than these he will do, because I go to My Father.

JOHN 14:12

PRAYER

HEAVENLY FATHER, *I choose to put my trust in You. You are my confidence, my hope, my source, and my victory. Nothing is impossible for You!*

I trust You to give me the strength and boldness I need to face every challenge I encounter today. I won't shrink back from my calling in You. I trust You to complete the good work You have started in my life!

In Jesus' name. **AMEN.**

I can do all things through Christ who strengthens me.

PHILIPPIANS 4:13

COURAGE

HEBREWS 11 lists some men and women in the Lord's "Hall of Faith." Each of these heroes exemplified bold faith in God that enabled them to take courage, even in very difficult circumstances.

We each need courage in order to fulfill God's purposes for our lives. We may not have to slay a giant (as David did), survive a den of hungry lions (as Daniel did), or lead people across the Red Sea (as Moses did), but we will surely need the same kind of courage and boldness to achieve the victory God has mapped out for our lives.

Whatever challenges you're facing today, remember this: You can be bold and strong, for God has promised to be with you!

Wait on the LORD. Be of good courage, and He shall strengthen your heart. Wait, I say, on the LORD!

PSALM 27:14

Be strong and of good courage; do not be afraid, nor be dismayed, for the LORD your God is with you wherever you go.

JOSHUA 1:9

When you pass through the waters, I will be with you; and through the rivers, they shall not overflow you. When you walk through the fire, you shall not be burned, nor shall the flame scorch you.

ISAIAH 43:2

Beloved, do not think it strange concerning the fiery trial which is to try you, as though some strange thing happened to you. But rejoice to the extent that you partake of Christ's sufferings, that when His glory is revealed, you may also be glad with exceeding joy.

1 PETER 4:12-13

I am persuaded that neither death nor life, nor angels nor principalities nor powers, nor things present nor things to come, nor height nor depth, nor any other created thing, shall be able to separate us from the love of God which is in Christ Jesus our Lord.

ROMANS 8:38-39

Be of good courage, and He shall strengthen your heart, all you who hope in the LORD.

PSALM 31:24

Have you not known? Have you not heard? The everlasting God, the LORD, the Creator of the ends of the earth, neither faints nor is weary. His understanding is unsearchable. He gives power to the weak, and to those who have no might He increases strength. Even the youths shall faint and be weary, and the young men shall utterly fall, but those who wait on the LORD shall renew their strength; they shall mount up with wings like eagles, they shall run and not be weary, they shall walk and not faint.

ISAIAH 40:28-31

Fear not, for I have redeemed you; I have called you by your name; you are Mine. When you pass through the waters, I will be with you; and through the rivers, they shall not overflow you. When you walk through the fire, you shall not be burned, nor shall the flame scorch you. For I am the LORD your God, the Holy One of Israel, your Savior.

ISAIAH 43:1-3

The eternal God is your refuge, and underneath are the everlasting arms. He will thrust out the enemy from before you, and will say, "Destroy!"

DEUTERONOMY 33:27

PRAYER

HEAVENLY FATHER, *I trust You to help me face the battles and storms in my life today. I choose to put my eyes on You and not on my circumstances. As I wait on You, I ask You to renew my strength and give me new vision for the overwhelming victory You desire to give me.*

Thank You for promising to be with me, no matter what challenges I may face today. I choose to rest in Your promise that nothing can separate me from Your love. I cast away all fear, and I trust You to give me Your strength and strategy for triumph in every area of my life.

In Jesus' name. **AMEN.**

The Lord is the Spirit; and where the Spirit of the Lord is, there is liberty.

2 CORINTHIANS 3:17

DELIVERANCE

GOD NEVER INTENDED for His people to be fearful or hesitant in dealing with Satan and the forces of darkness. The Gospels describe deliverance as a vital part of Jesus' ministry, and it is still a vital ministry today!

Jesus not only demonstrated the importance of preaching, teaching, and healing, but He also showed us the value of spiritual discernment, casting out demons, rebuking Satan, and taking authority over the powers of darkness.

We don't need to shrink back from this spiritual battle, for the Bible says God has given us the weapons and armor we need for victory. As you declare His Word over your life, God will deliver you from every chain and bondage—and He will bring you into His freedom!

The Spirit of the Lord is upon Me, because He has anointed Me to preach the gospel to the poor; He has sent Me to heal the broken-hearted, to proclaim liberty to the captives and recovery of sight to the blind, to set at liberty those who are oppressed; to proclaim the acceptable year of the Lord.

LUKE 4:18-19

For this purpose the Son of God was manifested, that He might destroy the works of the devil.

1 JOHN 3:8

You shall know the truth, and the truth shall make you free…Therefore if the Son makes you free, you shall be free indeed.

JOHN 8:32, 36

The law of the Spirit of life in Christ Jesus has made me free from the law of sin and death.

ROMANS 8:2

But now having been set free from sin, and having become slaves of God, you have your fruit to holiness, and the end, everlasting life.

ROMANS 6:22

Lord, even the demons are subject to us in Your name.

LUKE 10:17

Behold, I give you the authority to trample on serpents and scorpions, and over all the power of the enemy, and nothing shall by any means hurt you.

LUKE 10:19

They overcame (Satan)
by the blood of the Lamb
and by the word of their
testimony, and they
did not love their lives to
the death.

REVELATION 12:11

You are of God, little
children, and have overcome
them, because He who is in
you is greater than he who
is in the world.

1 JOHN 4:4

You are my hiding place;
You shall preserve me from
trouble; You shall surround
me with songs of deliverance.

PSALM 32:7

The LORD is my rock and
my fortress and my deliverer; the God of my strength,
in whom I will trust.

2 SAMUEL 22:2-3

I will say of the LORD,
"He is my refuge and my
fortress; my God, in Him I
will trust." Surely He shall
deliver you from the snare
of the fowler and from the
perilous pestilence.

PSALM 91:2-3

The Lord will deliver me
from every evil work and
preserve me for His heav-
enly kingdom. To Him be
glory forever and ever.

2 TIMOTHY 4:18

Do not lead us into temp-
tation, but deliver us from
the evil one. For Yours is the
kingdom and the power and
the glory forever.

MATTHEW 6:13

PRAYER

HEAVENLY FATHER, *thank You for sending Jesus to destroy the works of the devil and set spiritual captives free. Your Word says You've given Your people weapons and armor to overcome all the power of the enemy!*

I submit my life fully to You and ask You to reveal any demonic influence or bondage in my life. I repent of areas of sin that have given the enemy a foothold.

In Jesus' name, I rebuke any demon that would oppress, torment, or bind me or my loved ones. I declare freedom and deliverance in Jesus' mighty name! Thank You that Your Holy Spirit in me is more powerful than any satanic weapon formed against me.

In Jesus' name. **AMEN.**

*I will be merciful to their unrighteousness,
and their sins and their lawless deeds
I will remember no more.*

HEBREWS 8:12

ℱORGIVENESS

GOD WANTS TO SHOW YOU His forgiveness, and He wants you to know that, if you're in Christ, you're forgiven (1 John 5:11-12). Being forgiven in God's sight isn't a matter of good works, penance, or just trying harder—it's based on the work of Jesus on the Cross when He died for your sins!

Isaiah 53:6 says, *"All we like sheep have gone astray; we have turned, every one, to his own way; and the LORD has laid on [Jesus] the iniquity of us all."*

If you don't yet have assurance that you are forgiven and accepted by God, this can be your day for a new beginning! On the basis of God's Word, turn from any known sins in your life and ask Him to forgive you.

In Him we have redemption through His blood, the forgiveness of sins, according to the riches of His grace.

EPHESIANS 1:7

If anyone is in Christ, he is a new creation; old things have passed away; behold, all things have become new.

2 CORINTHIANS 5:17

Bless the LORD, O my soul, and forget not all His benefits: who forgives all your iniquities, who heals all your diseases, who redeems your life from destruction, who crowns you with lovingkindness and tender mercies, who satisfies your mouth with good things, so that your youth is renewed like the eagle's.

PSALM 103:2-5

I will cleanse them from all their iniquity by which they have sinned against Me, and I will pardon all their iniquities by which they have sinned and by which they have transgressed against Me.

JEREMIAH 33:8

If we confess our sins, He is faithful and just to forgive us our sins and to cleanse us from all unrighteousness.

1 JOHN 1:9

Let the wicked forsake his way, and the unrighteous man his thoughts. Let him return to the LORD, and He will have mercy on him; and to our God, for He will abundantly pardon.

ISAIAH 55:7

You have forgiven the iniquity of Your people; You have covered all their sin.
PSALM 85:2

You, being dead in your trespasses and the uncircumcision of your flesh, He has made alive together with Him, having forgiven you all trespasses.
COLOSSIANS 2:13

"Come now, and let us reason together," says the LORD, "Though your sins are like scarlet, they shall be as white as snow; though they are red like crimson, they shall be as wool."
ISAIAH 1:18

You will cast all our sins into the depths of the sea.
MICAH 7:19

The goodness of God leads you to repentance.
ROMANS 2:4

Blessed is he whose transgression is forgiven, whose sin is covered. Blessed is the man to whom the LORD does not impute iniquity, and in whose spirit there is no deceit.
PSALM 32:1-2

As far as the east is from the west, so far has He removed our transgressions from us.
PSALM 103:12

I have trusted in Your mercy; my heart shall rejoice in Your salvation. I will sing to the LORD, because He has dealt bountifully with me.
PSALM 13:5-6

PRAYER

HEAVENLY FATHER, *forgive me of my sins. Give me a fresh start and new beginning. I turn from anything that would hold me back from serving You.*

Thank You for sending Your Son Jesus to die for my sins. Thank You for coming into my heart and life to be my Lord. Fill me anew with Your Holy Spirit. Cleanse my heart and renew my conscience. Transform me into Your image!

In Jesus' name. **AMEN.**

GOD'S WILL

GOD HAS A GREAT PLAN for your life! In His will is our peace...our prosperity...our wholeness. Have you made this wonderful discovery yet? Are you living in the center of God's purpose for your life?

Finding God's will for your life is largely a matter of *trust*. When you really believe that God is all-wise and desires you to have an abundant life, you can trust yourself fully into His care.

In Jeremiah 29:11, the Lord speaks of His fantastic plans for you: *"'I know the thoughts that I think toward you,' says the LORD, 'thoughts of peace and not of evil, to give you a future and a hope.'"* No matter what your circumstances are today, God says He wants to give you a wonderful *"future and a hope."*

Trust in the LORD with all your heart, and lean not on your own understanding. In all your ways acknowledge Him, and He shall direct your paths.

PROVERBS 3:5-6

If any of you lacks wisdom, let him ask of God, who gives to all liberally and without reproach, and it will be given to him.

JAMES 1:5

This Book of the Law shall not depart from your mouth, but you shall meditate in it day and night, that you may observe to do according to all that is written in it. For then you will make your way prosperous, and then you will have good success.

JOSHUA 1:8

Your word is a lamp to my feet and a light to my path.

PSALM 119:105

Your ears shall hear a word behind you, saying, "This is the way, walk in it," whenever you turn to the right hand or whenever you turn to the left.

ISAIAH 30:21

This is God, our God forever and ever; He will be our guide even to death.

PSALM 48:14

The steps of a good man are ordered by the LORD, and He delights in his way.

PSALM 37:23

Commit your works to the LORD, and your thoughts will be established.

PROVERBS 16:3

You are my rock and my fortress; therefore, for Your name's sake, lead me and guide me.

PSALM 31:3

Thus says the LORD, your Redeemer, the Holy One of Israel: "I am the LORD your God, who teaches you to profit, who leads you by the way you should go."

ISAIAH 48:17

When He, the Spirit of truth, has come, He will guide you into all truth.

JOHN 16:13

The LORD will guide you continually, and satisfy your soul in drought, and strengthen your bones. You shall be like a watered garden, and like a spring of water, whose waters do not fail.

ISAIAH 58:11

The LORD is my shepherd; I shall not want. He makes me to lie down in green pastures; He leads me beside the still waters. He restores my soul; He leads me in the paths of righteousness for His name's sake.

PSALM 23:1-3

A man's heart plans his way, but the LORD directs his steps.

PROVERBS 16:9

PRAYER

LORD, *thank You for the great plans You have for my life! Instead of going my own way, I choose to trust You and follow You.*

I need Your wisdom, Lord. Show me Your ways. Teach me Your truth. Help me to hear the voice of Your Holy Spirit.

Thank You for being my Good Shepherd, always leading me in victory and blessing!

In Jesus' name. **AMEN.**

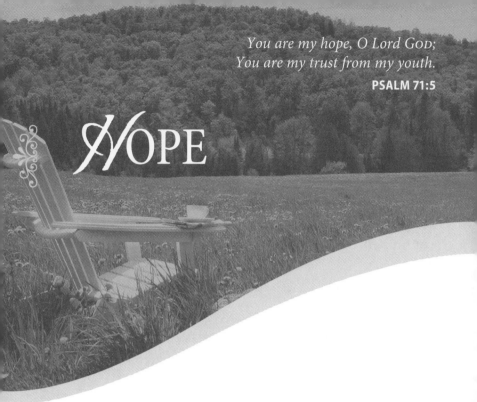

You are my hope, O Lord God;
You are my trust from my youth.

PSALM 71:5

*H*OPE

ONE DAY THE PROPHET JEREMIAH faced such difficult circumstances that he said despondently: *"My strength and my hope have perished from the LORD"* (Lamentations 3:18). Have *you* ever felt that way…as if you had no more strength or hope to face the difficult situations in your life?

The good news is that God restored Jeremiah's hope, reminding him that His compassion and faithfulness are *"new every morning"* (Lamentations 3:21-24). This can be your experience as well!

As you read the following verses, remember God's purpose in giving us His Word: *"…that we through the patience and comfort of the Scriptures might have hope"* (Romans 15:4). These truths of Scripture were written with *us* in mind!

Why are you cast down, O my soul? And why are you disquieted within me? Hope in God, for I shall yet praise Him for the help of His countenance.

PSALM 42:5

"I know the thoughts that I think toward you," says the LORD, "thoughts of peace and not of evil, to give you a future and a hope."

JEREMIAH 29:11

This I recall to my mind, therefore I have hope. Through the LORD's mercies we are not consumed, because His compassions fail not. They are new every morning; great is Your faithfulness. "The LORD is my portion," says my soul, "Therefore I hope in Him!"

LAMENTATIONS 3:21-24

I wait for the LORD, my soul waits, and in His word I do hope.

PSALM 130:5

Hope does not disappoint, because the love of God has been poured out in our hearts by the Holy Spirit who was given to us.

ROMANS 5:5

Let us hold fast the confession of our hope without wavering, for He who promised is faithful.

HEBREWS 10:23

God willed to make known what are the riches of the glory of this mystery among the Gentiles: which is Christ in you, the hope of glory.

COLOSSIANS 1:27

"There is hope in your future," says the LORD.

JEREMIAH 31:17

May the God of hope fill you with all joy and peace in believing, that you may abound in hope by the power of the Holy Spirit.

ROMANS 15:13

Hope in the LORD; for with the LORD there is mercy, and with Him is abundant redemption.

PSALM 130:7

Hope deferred makes the heart sick, but when the desire comes, it is a tree of life.

PROVERBS 13:12

Blessed is the man who trusts in the LORD, and whose hope is the LORD. For he shall be like a tree planted by the waters, which spreads out its roots by the river, and will not fear when heat comes; but its leaf will be green, and will not be anxious in the year of drought, nor will cease from yielding fruit.

JEREMIAH 17:7-8

This hope we have as an anchor of the soul, both sure and steadfast, and which enters the presence behind the veil.

HEBREWS 6:19

PRAYER

HEAVENLY FATHER, *thank You for being the God of Hope. I'm so grateful for the amazing promises in Your Word. I commit myself fully to You and trust You to work out Your purpose for my life.*

Forgive me, Lord, for looking to material things or other people for my hope, instead of fixing my eyes on You. Everything else in life may be shaken, but Your faithfulness remains.

I trust You as my steadfast Anchor during the storms of life. Lead me to Your victory and abundance, as Your Word promises!

In Jesus' name. **AMEN.**

*I waited patiently for the LORD; and He
inclined to me, and heard my cry.*

PSALM 40:1

PATIENCE

WHY IS IT SO DIFFICULT for us to be patient? Often it's because we want to be *in control* of a situation—to get our own way and get it NOW!

But the Bible says patience is an important character trait and fruit of the Holy Spirit. Patience comes from submitting our lives to Him and being filled with His Spirit. And it's a mark of God's love and His image in our lives.

The Bible says God will *reward* you when you set your heart to patiently wait on Him!

YOUR PROMISES *from* GOD'S WORD

The fruit of the Spirit is love, joy, peace, longsuffering [patience], kindness, goodness, faithfulness, gentleness, self-control.

GALATIANS 5:22-23

Those who wait on the LORD shall renew their strength; they shall mount up with wings like eagles, they shall run and not be weary, they shall walk and not faint.

ISAIAH 40:31

Wait on the LORD; be of good courage, and He shall strengthen your heart. Wait, I say, on the LORD!

PSALM 27:14

In returning and rest you shall be saved; in quietness and confidence shall be your strength.

ISAIAH 30:15

If we hope for what we do not see, we eagerly wait for it with perseverance.

ROMANS 8:25

Rest in the LORD, and wait patiently for Him; do not fret because of him who prospers in his way, because of the man who brings wicked schemes to pass. Cease from anger, and forsake wrath. Do not fret— it only causes harm. For evildoers shall be cut off; but those who wait on the LORD, they shall inherit the earth.

PSALM 37:7-9

The LORD is good to those who wait for Him, to the soul who seeks Him.

LAMENTATIONS 3:25

Do not become sluggish, but imitate those who through faith and patience inherit the promises.

HEBREWS 6:12

Knowing that the testing of your faith produces patience. But let patience have its perfect work, that you may be perfect and complete, lacking nothing.

JAMES 1:3-4

You have need of endurance, so that after you have done the will of God, you may receive the promise.

HEBREWS 10:36

The end of a thing is better than its beginning; the patient in spirit is better than the proud in spirit.

ECCLESIASTES 7:8

Be patient, brethren, until the coming of the Lord. See how the farmer waits for the precious fruit of the earth, waiting patiently for it until it receives the early and latter rain. You also be patient. Establish your hearts, for the coming of the Lord is at hand.

JAMES 5:7-8

We also glory in tribulations, knowing that tribulation produces perseverance; and perseverance, character; and character, hope. Now hope does not disappoint, because the love of God has been poured out in our hearts by the Holy Spirit who was given to us.

ROMANS 5:3-5

PRAYER

HEAVENLY FATHER, *thank You for always being patient with me. Forgive me for so often being in a hurry to get my own way, rather than serving others and waiting on You.*

I trust You to answer my prayers in Your time and in Your way. Your Word says You'll fulfill all Your promises when I come to You in both faith and patience. As I plant seeds of faith, I trust You to give me a bountiful harvest of Your blessings!

Forgive me for being impatient with others. May I be patient with them as You are patient with me.

In Jesus' name. **AMEN.**

*The meek shall inherit the earth,
and shall delight themselves
in the abundance of peace.*

PSALM 37:11

PEACE

PEOPLE LOOK FOR PEACE in so many places: relationships, recreation, drugs, sex, exercise, and meditation, just to name a few. Yet the Bible says the only source of lasting peace is in Jesus, the *"Prince of Peace"* (Isaiah 9:6). Everything else passes away, but His peace stands the test of time and eternity.

Are you experiencing this amazing peace with God? The Bible says it begins when you're *"justified by faith"* and know He has forgiven you (Romans 5:1). Because of what Jesus did on the Cross for you, you can live in the reality of His peace, which is beyond our understanding (Philippians 4:7).

You will keep him in perfect peace, whose mind is stayed on You, because he trusts in You.

ISAIAH 26:3

Peace I leave with you, My peace I give to you; not as the world gives do I give to you. Let not your heart be troubled, neither let it be afraid.

JOHN 14:27

Be anxious for nothing, but in everything by prayer and supplication, with thanksgiving, let your requests be made known to God; and the peace of God, which surpasses all understanding, will guard your hearts and minds through Christ Jesus.

PHILIPPIANS 4:6-7

Having been justified by faith, we have peace with God through our Lord Jesus Christ.

ROMANS 5:1

LORD, You will establish peace for us, for You have also done all our works in us.

ISAIAH 26:12

You shall go out with joy, and be led out with peace; the mountains and the hills shall break forth into singing before you, and all the trees of the field shall clap their hands.

ISAIAH 55:12

To be carnally minded is death, but to be spiritually minded is life and peace.

ROMANS 8:6

The LORD bless you and keep you; the LORD make His face shine upon you, and be gracious to you; the LORD lift up His countenance upon you, and give you peace.

NUMBERS 6:24-26

Great peace have those who love Your law, and nothing causes them to stumble.

PSALM 119:165

The kingdom of God is not eating and drinking, but righteousness and peace and joy in the Holy Spirit. For he who serves Christ in these things is acceptable to God and approved by men. Therefore let us pursue the things which make for peace and the things by which one may edify another.

ROMANS 14:17-19

Finally, brethren, farewell. Become complete. Be of good comfort, be of one mind, live in peace; and the God of love and peace will be with you.

2 CORINTHIANS 13:11

May the God of hope fill you with all joy and peace in believing, that you may abound in hope by the power of the Holy Spirit.

ROMANS 15:13

I will both lie down in peace, and sleep; for You alone, O LORD, make me dwell in safety.

PSALM 4:8

PRAYER

FATHER, *thank You for purchasing my peace on the Cross, so that I can come boldly into Your presence as Your friend!*

Lead me by Your peace. I cast all my cares on You. I trust You to accomplish Your purpose for my life.

Bring to light any areas of my heart that are causing me to sacrifice Your peace and fall short of Your great plans for me. Reign in my life as my Lord and Savior!

In Jesus' name. **AMEN.**

> *He will guard the feet of His saints, but the wicked shall be silent in darkness. For by strength no man shall prevail.*
>
> **1 SAMUEL 2:9**

$\mathcal{P}$ROTECTION

DO YOU FEEL UNDER ATTACK TODAY? The Bible describes a very real spiritual battle that rages against us in the unseen realm. The devil is an enemy intent on doing us harm, but the good news today is that God promises to defend and protect those who put their trust in Him.

The Bible declares that God has prepared a place of safety for you. The enemy's onslaught may continue for a while longer, but God beckons you to a safe haven in His presence.

Whatever personal storm you are facing today, God's strength is greater, and He offers to bring you to His place of shelter and provision.

My sheep hear My voice, and I know them, and they follow Me. And I give them eternal life, and they shall never perish; neither shall anyone snatch them out of My hand. My Father, who has given them to Me, is greater than all; and no one is able to snatch them out of My Father's hand.

JOHN 10:27-29

When you pass through the waters, I will be with you; and through the rivers, they shall not overflow you. When you walk through the fire, you shall not be burned, nor shall the flame scorch you.

ISAIAH 43:2

The God of Israel will be your rear guard.

ISAIAH 52:12

If God is for us, who can be against us? In all these things we are more than conquerors through Him who loved us.

ROMANS 8:31, 37

You, O LORD, are a shield for me, my glory and the One who lifts up my head.

PSALM 3:3

If you indeed obey His voice and do all that I speak, then I will be an enemy to your enemies and an adversary to your adversaries.

EXODUS 23:22

The peace of God, which surpasses all understanding, will guard your hearts and minds through Christ Jesus.

PHILIPPIANS 4:7

As the mountains surround Jerusalem, so the LORD surrounds His people from this time forth and forever.

PSALM 125:2

The eternal God is your refuge, and underneath are the everlasting arms; He will thrust out the enemy from before you.

DEUTERONOMY 33:27

A thousand may fall at your side, and ten thousand at your right hand; but it shall not come near you.

PSALM 91:7

You have been a shelter for me, a strong tower from the enemy.

PSALM 61:3

The LORD your God, who goes before you, He will fight for you.

DEUTERONOMY 1:30

Do not be afraid nor dismayed…for the battle is not yours, but God's.

2 CHRONICLES 20:15

The Lord is faithful, who will establish you and guard you from the evil one.

2 THESSALONIANS 3:3

I know whom I have believed and am persuaded that He is able to keep what I have committed to Him until that Day.

2 TIMOTHY 1:12

PRAYER

HEAVENLY FATHER, *Your Word promises I can run to You and find safety. You're my strength and refuge during all the storms of life. Help me keep my eyes on You instead of my circumstances.*

You have promised to be an enemy to my enemies as I live in a covenant relationship with You. Just as the Israelites were protected by the blood of the lamb they placed on the doorposts of their houses during Passover, I claim the blood of Jesus today as protection against the devil's attacks on me or my loved ones.

I declare today that You are a mighty warrior in my defense. You've given me the weapons and armor I need for victory in every situation!

In Jesus' name. **AMEN.**

*Whatever things you ask in prayer,
believing, you will receive.*

MATTHEW 21:22

PROVISION

YOU HAVE A Heavenly Father who wants His children to prosper! Yes, there can be tough times along the way. But God wants you to trust Him and learn His principles for financial blessings.

Don't allow fear to paralyze you or make you passive today. Step out in faith to obey God's leading, and plant financial seeds that He can use to bring you a great harvest of blessings in the days to come.

Remember: God wants to be your covenant partner in every area of your life. The Bible promises: *"Those who seek the Lord shall not lack **any** good thing!"* (Psalm 34:10).

God is able to make all grace abound toward you, that you, always having all sufficiency in all things, may have an abundance for every good work.

2 CORINTHIANS 9:8

My God shall supply all your need according to His riches in glory by Christ Jesus.

PHILIPPIANS 4:19

His divine power has given to us all things that pertain to life and godliness, through the knowledge of Him who called us by glory and virtue.

2 PETER 1:3

Let the LORD be magnified, Who has pleasure in the prosperity of His servant.

PSALM 35:27

Seek first the kingdom of God and His righteousness, and all these things shall be added to you.

MATTHEW 6:33

The young lions lack and suffer hunger; but those who seek the LORD shall not lack any good thing.

PSALM 34:10

"Bring all the tithes into the storehouse, that there may be food in My house, and try Me now in this," says the LORD of hosts, "If I will not open for you the windows of heaven and pour out for you such blessing that there will not be room enough to receive it. And I will rebuke the devourer for your sakes."

MALACHI 3:10-11

Give, and it will be given to you: good measure, pressed down, shaken together, and running over will be put into your bosom. For with the same measure that you use, it will be measured back to you.

LUKE 6:38

The LORD will command the blessing on you in your storehouses and in all to which you set your hand, and He will bless you in the land which the LORD your God is giving you...The LORD will open to you His good treasure, the heavens, to give the rain to your land in its season, and to bless all the work of your hand. You shall lend to many nations, but you shall not borrow.

DEUTERONOMY 28:8, 12

He who did not spare His own Son, but delivered Him up for us all, how shall He not with Him also freely give us all things?

ROMANS 8:32

You shall remember the LORD your God, for it is He who gives you power to get wealth, that He may establish His covenant which He swore to your fathers, as it is this day.

DEUTERONOMY 8:18

As the eyes of servants look to the hand of their masters, as the eyes of a maid to the hand of her mistress, so our eyes look to the LORD our God.

PSALM 123:2

PRAYER

HEAVENLY FATHER, *I declare You to be my covenant partner and the rightful owner of everything I have. I call on You to fulfill Your Word, opening the windows of Heaven and pouring out overflowing abundance in my life. Rebuke the enemy and keep him from stealing, killing, or destroying the blessings You intend for me.*

Instead of shrinking back in fear and unbelief, I choose to trust You with my finances. I want to take steps of faith and sow financial seeds that will result in a great harvest of Your provision.

Father, I seek Your Kingdom and Your righteousness. As You bless me, I pledge that I will be a blessing to others. I want to abound for every good work You've planned for me!

In Jesus' name. **AMEN.**

GOD'S PROMISES
for
WHEN YOU FEEL...

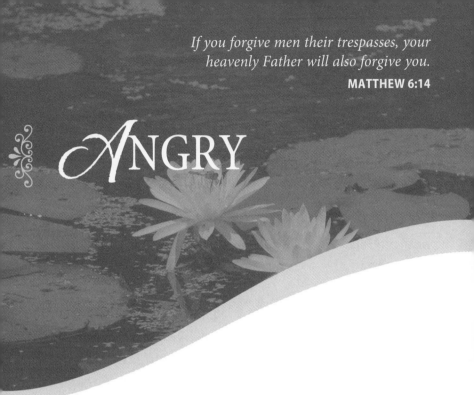

If you forgive men their trespasses, your heavenly Father will also forgive you.

MATTHEW 6:14

ANGRY

THE BIBLE is filled with warnings about the destructive qualities of uncontrolled anger, and several of the *"works of the flesh"* listed in Galatians 5:19-21 are anger related: *"outbursts of wrath"* and *"murders."*

In contrast to such negative deeds, the apostle Paul lists the *"fruit of the Spirit,"* which are powerful antidotes to the self-centered anger the Bible warns about: *"love, joy, peace, longsuffering, kindness, goodness, faithfulness, gentleness, self-control"* (Galatians 5:22-23).

Paul says we are to *"put off...anger, wrath, malice..."* and *"put on love, which is the bond of perfection"* (Colossians 3:8-14).

My beloved brethren, let every man be swift to hear, slow to speak, slow to wrath; for the wrath of man does not produce the righteousness of God.

JAMES 1:19-20

Be angry, and do not sin: do not let the sun go down on your wrath.

EPHESIANS 4:26

Let all bitterness, wrath, anger, clamor, and evil speaking be put away from you, with all malice. And be kind to one another, tenderhearted, forgiving one another, even as God in Christ forgave you.

EPHESIANS 4:31-32

A soft answer turns away wrath, but a harsh word stirs up anger.

PROVERBS 15:1

Beloved, do not avenge yourselves, but rather give place to wrath; for it is written, "Vengeance is Mine, I will repay," says the Lord. Therefore, "If your enemy is hungry, feed him; if he is thirsty, give him a drink. For in so doing you will heap coals of fire on his head." Do not be overcome by evil, but overcome evil with good.

ROMANS 12:19-21

Cease from anger, and forsake wrath; do not fret— it only causes harm.

PSALM 37:8

He who is slow to anger is better than the mighty, and he who rules his spirit than he who takes a city.

PROVERBS 16:32

But I say to you that whoever is angry with his brother without a cause shall be in danger of the judgment. And whoever says to his brother, "Raca!" shall be in danger of the council. But whoever says, "You fool!" shall be in danger of hell fire. Therefore if you bring your gift to the altar, and there remember that your brother has something against you, leave your gift there before the altar, and go your way. First be reconciled to your brother, and then come and offer your gift.

MATTHEW 5:22-24

A wise man fears and departs from evil, but a fool rages and is self-confident. A quick-tempered man acts foolishly, and a man of wicked intentions is hated.

PROVERBS 14:16-17

Where envy and self-seeking exist, confusion and every evil thing are there. But the wisdom that is from above is first pure, then peaceable, gentle, willing to yield, full of mercy and good fruits, without partiality and without hypocrisy. Now the fruit of righteousness is sown in peace by those who make peace.

JAMES 3:16-18

PRAYER

HEAVENLY FATHER, *I want You to be Lord of my every thought, emotion, and action. Fill me with Your Holy Spirit and let His fruit be manifested in everything I say or do.*

Forgive me for the ways I've allowed anger to be a destructive force in my life in the past. Help me bring healing to any relationships that have been damaged by my angry words or deeds.

Teach me self-control, Lord, and help me walk in Your love and forgiveness in every situation.

In Jesus' name. **AMEN.**

The Lord will perfect that which concerns me.

PSALM 138:8

ANXIOUS

GOD DOESN'T PROMISE us a carefree life, but He says we can cast all our cares upon Him (1 Peter 5:7). Much of the anxiety we experience is the result of trying to shoulder life's burdens in our own strength instead of His. Since the government of the whole universe is on the Lord's shoulders (Isaiah 9:6), He surely can handle your cares as well!

The Bible encourages you to experience peace and security in His love today: *"The beloved of the LORD shall dwell in safety by Him, who shelters him all the day long; and he shall dwell between His shoulders"* (Deuteronomy 33:12). Put your trust fully in the Lord, and know that you can rest safely in His love!

Let the peace of God rule in your hearts...and be thankful.
COLOSSIANS 3:15

Be anxious for nothing, but in everything by prayer and supplication, with thanksgiving, let your requests be made known to God; and the peace of God, which surpasses all understanding, will guard your hearts and minds through Christ Jesus.
PHILIPPIANS 4:6-7

Casting all your care upon Him, for He cares for you.
1 PETER 5:7

You will keep him in perfect peace, whose mind is stayed on You, because he trusts in You.
ISAIAH 26:3

I will both lie down in peace, and sleep; for You alone, O LORD, make me dwell in safety.
PSALM 4:8

Great peace have those who love Your law, and nothing causes them to stumble.
PSALM 119:165

Cast your burden on the LORD, and He shall sustain you; He shall never permit the righteous to be moved.
PSALM 55:22

He who dwells in the secret place of the Most High shall abide under the shadow of the Almighty. I will say of the LORD, "He is my refuge and my fortress; my God, in Him I will trust."
PSALM 91:1-2

Therefore I say to you, do not worry about your life, what you will eat or what you will drink; nor about your body, what you will put on. Is not life more than food and the body more than clothing? Look at the birds of the air, for they neither sow nor reap nor gather into barns; yet your heavenly Father feeds them. Are you not of more value than they?…

Therefore do not worry, saying, "What shall we eat?" or "What shall we drink?" or "What shall we wear?" For after all these things the Gentiles seek. For your heavenly Father knows that you need all these things. But seek first the kingdom of God and His righteousness, and all these things shall be added to you.

Therefore do not worry about tomorrow, for tomorrow will worry about its own things. Sufficient for the day is its own trouble.

MATTHEW 6:25-34

Rest in the LORD, and wait patiently for Him; do not fret because of him who prospers in his way, because of the man who brings wicked schemes to pass. Cease from anger, and forsake wrath; do not fret—it only causes harm.

PSALM 37:7-8

Though I walk in the midst of trouble, You will revive me; You will stretch out Your hand against the wrath of my enemies, and Your right hand will save me. The LORD will perfect that which concerns me.

PSALM 138:7-8

PRAYER

HEAVENLY FATHER, *forgive me for trying to carry life's challenges on my own shoulders. I cast all my cares on You today, recognizing that You care for me.*

I fix my eyes on You instead of my problems, Lord. Quiet my restless heart, and teach me to rest confidently in Your peace and security. I draw near to abide in Your secret place. Be my refuge and fortress as I put my trust in You.

Thank You, Lord, for giving me all the grace I need for this day. I trust tomorrow into Your hands, knowing You will be with me every step of the way.

In Jesus' name. **AMEN.**

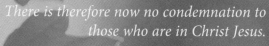

There is therefore now no condemnation to those who are in Christ Jesus.

ROMANS 8:1

CONDEMNED

THE BIBLE describes Satan as *"the accuser"* (Revelation 12:10-11), so it shouldn't be surprising that he takes delight in sowing feelings of condemnation among God's people. He accuses us *"day and night,"* doing everything possible to make us feel unaccepted by God.

Fortunately, this same passage tells how we can overcome Satan's accusations: *"They overcame him by the blood of the Lamb and by the word of their testimony, and they did not love their lives to the death."*

Because of Jesus' blood shed for us on the Cross, we can receive God's grace and forgiveness instead of Satan's condemnation and fear. We can testify that Satan is a liar, and God's promises are true in our lives!

He has not dealt with us according to our sins, nor punished us according to our iniquities…As far as the east is from the west, so far has He removed our transgressions from us.

PSALM 103:10, 12

God did not send His Son into the world to condemn the world, but that the world through Him might be saved. He who believes in Him is not condemned; but he who does not believe is condemned already, because he has not believed in the name of the only begotten Son of God.

JOHN 3:17-18

You will cast all our sins into the depths of the sea.

MICAH 7:19

If anyone is in Christ, he is a new creation; old things have passed away; behold, all things have become new.

2 CORINTHIANS 5:17

Most assuredly, I say to you, he who hears My word and believes in Him who sent Me has everlasting life, and shall not come into judgment, but has passed from death into life.

JOHN 5:24

Let the wicked forsake his way, and the unrighteous man his thoughts. Let him return to the LORD, and He will have mercy on him; and to our God, for He will abundantly pardon.

ISAIAH 55:7

If we confess our sins, He is faithful and just to forgive us our sins and to cleanse us from all unrighteousness.

1 JOHN 1:9

When Jesus had raised Himself up and saw no one but the woman, He said to her, "Woman, where are those accusers of yours? Has no one condemned you?" She said, "No one, Lord." And Jesus said to her, "Neither do I condemn you; go and sin no more."

JOHN 8:10-11

Let us draw near with a true heart in full assurance of faith, having our hearts sprinkled from an evil conscience and our bodies washed with pure water.

HEBREWS 10:22

The LORD your God is gracious and merciful, and will not turn His face from you if you return to Him.

2 CHRONICLES 30:9

They overcame [the devil, the accuser] by the blood of the Lamb and by the word of their testimony.

REVELATION 12:11

If anyone sins, we have an Advocate with the Father, Jesus Christ the righteous. And He Himself is the propitiation for our sins, and not for ours only but also for the whole world.

1 JOHN 2:1-2

PRAYER

HEAVENLY FATHER, *I declare that Your Word is true: Jesus' blood has set me free from condemnation, fear, and death. Instead of allowing me to wallow in torment and defeat, You've made me an overcomer!*

Thank You for showing me Satan is a liar and the father of lies (John 8:44). The truth is that You love me and sent Your Son to purchase my forgiveness and freedom. In Him I'm a new creation. You've made all things new!

Father, help me to keep my eyes on You and continually celebrate Your grace and forgiveness. I will stand firm in this new liberty!

In Jesus' name. **AMEN.**

CONFUSED

OUR ENGLISH WORD "CONFUSE" comes from a Latin word that means "to mix together." And that's exactly what confusion is—a mixture of truth and error, God's Word and Satan's lies.

God doesn't want us to be confused! He gave us the Bible so we would know the truth, and He promised that the truth would set us free (John 8:32)—free from the enemy's lies, and free from confusion!

Instead of being confused by all the swirling opinions of this world, God says you can *"be transformed by the renewing of your mind"* (Romans 12:2). That happens when you actively replace any lies you've believed with the truth of God's Word!

God has not given us a spirit of fear, but of power and of love and of a sound mind.

2 TIMOTHY 1:7

Beloved, do not think it strange concerning the fiery trial which is to try you, as though some strange thing happened to you; but rejoice to the extent that you partake of Christ's sufferings, that when His glory is revealed, you may also be glad with exceeding joy.

1 PETER 4:12-13

Your ears shall hear a word behind you, saying, "This is the way, walk in it," whenever you turn to the right hand or whenever you turn to the left.

ISAIAH 30:21

Where envy and self-seeking exist, confusion and every evil thing are there. But the wisdom that is from above is first pure, then peaceable, gentle, willing to yield, full of mercy and good fruits, without partiality and without hypocrisy.

JAMES 3:16-17

Trust in the LORD with all your heart, and lean not on your own understanding. In all your ways acknowledge Him, and He shall direct your paths.

PROVERBS 3:5-6

Let the peace of God rule in your hearts.

COLOSSIANS 3:15

I will instruct you and teach you in the way you should go; I will guide you with My eye.

PSALM 32:8

Great peace have those who love Your law, and nothing causes them to stumble.

PSALM 119:165

Cast your burden on the LORD, and He shall sustain you; He shall never permit the righteous to be moved.

PSALM 55:22

We have the mind of Christ.

1 CORINTHIANS 2:16

Be anxious for nothing, but in everything by prayer and supplication, with thanksgiving, let your requests be made known to God; and the peace of God, which surpasses all understanding, will guard your hearts and minds through Christ Jesus.

PHILIPPIANS 4:6-7

If any of you lacks wisdom, let him ask of God, who gives to all liberally and without reproach, and it will be given to him. But let him ask in faith, with no doubting, for he who doubts is like a wave of the sea driven and tossed by the wind. For let not that man suppose that he will receive anything from the Lord; he is a double-minded man, unstable in all his ways.

JAMES 1:5-8

PRAYER

HEAVENLY FATHER, *You are the author of peace and not confusion. Calm the raging storms in my life, and shine the light of Your presence into every troubled crevice of my mind.*

Today I embrace Your Word as truth, and I renounce the confusion and lies sown by the enemy. Lead me by Your peace and joy. Renew my mind so I see things from Your perspective.

Teach me Your ways, Lord. Let me discern Your voice in the midst of so many competing voices and opinions. I declare that You are my Lord and my God!

In Jesus' name. **AMEN.**

DEPRESSED

DEPRESSION IS OFTEN a reaction to the difficult circumstances, trials, and temptations of life—things like marital problems, wayward children, financial pressures, or sickness. Physical causes such as fatigue or chemical imbalances can also contribute to our downward spiral, causing us to feel helpless and unable to cope with our situation.

Sometimes depression stems from a direct spiritual attack from the devil, who wants to sow seeds of unbelief and steal our joy (John 10:10). And we must be careful not to give the enemy a foothold through some area of sin or disobedience in our life.

The heroes in the Bible were no different. Like us, they encountered times when they had to overcome discouragement and depression. Yet they found victory by bringing their feelings to the Lord and asking for His joy to be restored in their lives (Psalm 51:12). This can be *your* testimony as well!

Why are you cast down, O my soul? And why are you disquieted within me? Hope in God, for I shall yet praise Him for the help of His countenance.

PSALM 42:5

When you pass through the waters, I will be with you; and through the rivers, they shall not overflow you. When you walk through the fire, you shall not be burned, nor shall the flame scorch you.

ISAIAH 43:2

Fear not, for I am with you; be not dismayed, for I am your God. I will strengthen you, yes, I will help you, I will uphold you with My righteous right hand.

ISAIAH 41:10

He spoke a parable to them, that men always ought to pray and not lose heart.

LUKE 18:1

This day is holy to our LORD. Do not sorrow, for the joy of the LORD is your strength.

NEHEMIAH 8:10

His anger is but for a moment, His favor is for life. Weeping may endure for a night, but joy comes in the morning.

PSALM 30:5

Those who wait on the LORD shall renew their strength; they shall mount up with wings like eagles, they shall run and not be weary, they shall walk and not faint.

ISAIAH 40:31

DEPRESSED

Humble yourselves under the mighty hand of God, that He may exalt you in due time, casting all your care upon Him, for He cares for you.

1 PETER 5:6-7

The ransomed of the LORD shall return, and come to Zion with singing, with everlasting joy on their heads. They shall obtain joy and gladness; sorrow and sighing shall flee away.

ISAIAH 51:11

To console those who mourn in Zion, to give them beauty for ashes, the oil of joy for mourning, the garment of praise for the spirit of heaviness; that they may be called trees of righteousness, the planting of the LORD, that He may be glorified.

ISAIAH 61:3

Blessed be the God and Father of our Lord Jesus Christ, the Father of mercies and God of all comfort, who comforts us in all our tribulation, that we may be able to comfort those who are in any trouble, with the comfort with which we ourselves are comforted by God.

2 CORINTHIANS 1:3-4

Finally, brethren, whatever things are true, whatever things are noble, whatever things are just, whatever things are pure, whatever things are lovely, whatever things are of good report, if there is any virtue and if there is anything praiseworthy—meditate on these things.

PHILIPPIANS 4:8

PRAYER

FATHER, *I thank You today that You are with me and You love me even when I'm feeling down. You are able to turn my sadness into dancing, replacing my depression with the joy that comes from being in Your presence. I choose to cast aside every worry, fear, doubt, and depressing thought from my mind, allowing You to replace them with Your peace.*

I declare that Satan has no right to control my thoughts. Instead of negative thoughts, I choose to set my mind on Your Word and Your promises of victory.

Lord, I come into Your presence, where there is fullness of joy. Renew my strength as I wait upon You, and help me to mount up with wings like an eagle.

In Jesus' name. **AMEN.**

Let not your heart be troubled; you believe in God, believe also in Me.

JOHN 14:1

DISCOURAGED

ONE OF THE DEVIL'S most successful tactics is to sow discouragement into our lives. "Dis-couragement" literally means that we are robbed of our courage... our endurance...our joy...and our hope.

Has the enemy robbed you today? If so, the Lord wants to restore what you've lost. He wants to restore your joy and draw you closer to Him than you've ever been before.

Many of the greatest Believers who have ever lived faced discouragement at some point in their lives. David cried out to the Lord, *"Restore to me the joy of Your salvation!"* (Psalm 51:12), and perhaps that is your prayer as well. If so, God's Word says you can find *"fullness of joy"* in His presence (Psalm 16:11)!

Brethren, whatever things are true, whatever things are noble, whatever things are just, whatever things are pure, whatever things are lovely, whatever things are of good report, if there is any virtue and if there is anything praiseworthy— meditate on these things.

PHILIPPIANS 4:8

Be of good courage, and He shall strengthen your heart, all you who hope in the LORD.

PSALM 31:24

We were burdened beyond measure, above strength, so that we despaired even of life…that we should not trust in ourselves but in God who raises the dead.

2 CORINTHIANS 1:8-9

Peace I leave with you, My peace I give to you; not as the world gives do I give to you. Let not your heart be troubled, neither let it be afraid.

JOHN 14:27

We are hard-pressed on every side, yet not crushed; we are perplexed, but not in despair; persecuted, but not forsaken; struck down, but not destroyed.

2 CORINTHIANS 4:8-9

Do not cast away your confidence, which has great reward. For you have need of endurance, so that after you have done the will of God, you may receive the promise.

HEBREWS 10:35-36

Being confident of this very thing, that He who has begun a good work in you will complete it until the day of Jesus Christ.

PHILIPPIANS 1:6

Let us not grow weary while doing good, for in due season we shall reap if we do not lose heart.

GALATIANS 6:9

Though I walk in the midst of trouble, You will revive me; You will stretch out Your hand against the wrath of my enemies, and Your right hand will save me.

PSALM 138:7

Weeping may endure for a night, but joy comes in the morning.

PSALM 30:5

In the time of trouble He shall hide me in His pavilion; in the secret place of His tabernacle He shall hide me; He shall set me high upon a rock. And now my head shall be lifted up above my enemies all around me. Therefore I will offer sacrifices of joy in His tabernacle; I will sing, yes, I will sing praises to the LORD…I would have lost heart, unless I had believed that I would see the goodness of the LORD in the land of the living. Wait on the LORD; be of good courage, and He shall strengthen your heart. Wait, I say, on the LORD!

PSALM 27:5-6, 13-14

PRAYER

FATHER, *I put my trust in You. Restore my joy and courage today! I cast away my heaviness and ask You to fill me afresh with Your Spirit.*

My hope is not in my own ability but in Your supernatural power. My eyes are on You rather than on my circumstances. I let go of the disappointments of the past and trust my present and future to You.

Thank You for being with me in every situation. Thank You for lifting me up when I fall. I trust You to fulfill Your purpose for my life!

In Jesus' name. **AMEN.**

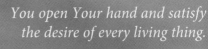

*D*ISSATISFIED

OFTEN WE BECOME frustrated and discouraged in our Christian life when we try to live it in our own strength. That is not God's plan! The only way we can successfully live the Christian life is to allow Christ to live HIS life through us! That's why the apostle Paul wrote: *"It is no longer I who live, but Christ lives in me"* (Galatians 2:20).

If you're dissatisfied with your Christian life today, ask yourself if you're truly allowing Christ to live His supernatural life through you by the Holy Spirit. On the one hand, Jesus warns, *"Without Me you can do nothing"* (John 15:5), but Paul points out the other side of the coin: *"I can do all things through Christ who strengthens me"* (Philippians 4:13).

You don't need to remain frustrated or dissatisfied. Let God give you new vision and restore your joy today!

The young lions lack and suffer hunger; but those who seek the LORD shall not lack any good thing.

PSALM 34:10

I have learned in whatever state I am, to be content: I know how to be abased, and I know how to abound. Everywhere and in all things I have learned both to be full and to be hungry, both to abound and to suffer need. I can do all things through Christ who strengthens me.

PHILIPPIANS 4:11-13

You shall eat in plenty and be satisfied, and praise the name of the LORD your God, who has dealt wondrously with you; and My people shall never be put to shame.

JOEL 2:26

O God, You are my God; early will I seek You; my soul thirsts for You; my flesh longs for You in a dry and thirsty land where there is no water. So I have looked for You in the sanctuary, to see Your power and Your glory. Because Your lovingkindness is better than life, my lips shall praise You. Thus I will bless You while I live; I will lift up my hands in Your name. My soul shall be satisfied as with marrow and fatness, and my mouth shall praise You with joyful lips.

PSALM 63:1-5

God is able to make all grace abound toward you, that you, always having all sufficiency in all things, may have an abundance for every good work.

2 CORINTHIANS 9:8

Ho! Everyone who thirsts, come to the waters; and you who have no money, come, buy and eat. Yes, come, buy wine and milk without money and without price.

ISAIAH 55:1

Blessed are those who hunger and thirst for righteousness, for they shall be filled.

MATTHEW 5:6

How precious is Your lovingkindness, O God! Therefore the children of men put their trust under the shadow of Your wings. They are abundantly satisfied with the fullness of Your house, and You give them drink from the river of Your pleasures.

PSALM 36:7-8

Bless the LORD, O my soul; and all that is within me, bless His holy name! Bless the LORD, O my soul, and forget not all His benefits: who forgives all your iniquities, who heals all your diseases, who redeems your life from destruction, who crowns you with lovingkindness and tender mercies, who satisfies your mouth with good things, so that your youth is renewed like the eagle's.

PSALM 103:1-5

He satisfies the longing soul, and fills the hungry soul with goodness.

PSALM 107:9

PRAYER

LORD, *I ask You to restore the joy of my salvation.
Give me a grateful heart for all You've done for me.
I repent of grumbling!*

*In Your presence is fullness of joy. At Your right hand are
pleasures forevermore. Remove anything from my heart
that hinders my intimacy with You. Fill me with Your Spirit
and live Your supernatural life through me.*

*Teach me contentment, Lord, so that I can rejoice
in You in every situation!*

In Jesus' name. **AMEN.**

God has not given us a spirit of fear, but of power and of love and of a sound mind.

2 TIMOTHY 1:7

FEARFUL

IN MANY WAYS, *fear* is simply *faith* that is focused in the wrong direction. Instead of seeing God's love and His power to protect us, fear causes our attention to be consumed with the problems arrayed against us. The challenges we face seem bigger than the Lord—a sure sign our faith has been misplaced.

What are you afraid of today? No doubt it seems very real and very troubling. But the Bible asks a powerful question: *"If God is for us, who can be against us?"* (Romans 8:31). The Lord wants you to know that *whatever* situation is coming against you today, He is bigger!

Take a few moments right now and change your focus. Put your faith in God instead of in your problems. Fix your eyes on Jesus, for He is *"the author and perfecter of our faith"* (Hebrews 12:2).

You did not receive the spirit of bondage again to fear, but you received the Spirit of adoption by whom we cry out, "Abba, Father."

ROMANS 8:15

He shall cover you with His feathers, and under His wings you shall take refuge; His truth shall be your shield and buckler. You shall not be afraid of the terror by night, nor of the arrow that flies by day, nor of the pestilence that walks in darkness, nor of the destruction that lays waste at noonday. A thousand may fall at your side, and ten thousand at your right hand; but it shall not come near you.

PSALM 91:4-7

Fear not, for I am with you.

ISAIAH 41:10

In God I have put my trust; I will not be afraid. What can man do to me?

PSALM 56:11

There is no fear in love; but perfect love casts out fear, because fear involves torment. But he who fears has not been made perfect in love.

1 JOHN 4:18

No evil shall befall you, nor shall any plague come near your dwelling; for He shall give His angels charge over you, to keep you in all your ways.

PSALM 91:10-11

I sought the LORD, and He heard me, and delivered me from all my fears.

PSALM 34:4

Yea, though I walk through the valley of the shadow of death, I will fear no evil; for You are with me; Your rod and Your staff, they comfort me. You prepare a table before me in the presence of my enemies; You anoint my head with oil; my cup runs over.

PSALM 23:4-5

Who shall separate us from the love of Christ? Shall tribulation, or distress, or persecution, or famine, or nakedness, or peril, or sword? As it is written: "For Your sake we are killed all day long; we are accounted as sheep for the slaughter." Yet in all these things we are more than conquerors through Him who loved us. For I am persuaded that neither death nor life, nor angels nor principalities nor powers, nor things present nor things to come, nor height nor depth, nor any other created thing, shall be able to separate us from the love of God which is in Christ Jesus our Lord.

ROMANS 8:35-39

Peace I leave with you, My peace I give to you; not as the world gives do I give to you. Let not your heart be troubled, neither let it be afraid.

JOHN 14:27

The LORD is my light and my salvation; whom shall I fear? The LORD is the strength of my life; of whom shall I be afraid?

PSALM 27:1

PRAYER

HEAVENLY FATHER, *forgive me for focusing more on my problems than I've been focusing on You. I look to You today to fill me with Your love and free me from fear.*

Thank You for Your promise to fight my battles for me and give me victory over my enemies. Thank You for replacing my fear with Your perfect peace.

Thank You for promising to be with me even in the dark valleys of life. I trust You to keep me safe in every situation!

In Jesus' name. **AMEN.**

The eternal God is your refuge, and underneath are the everlasting arms.

DEUTERONOMY 33:27

LONELY

LONELINESS can be a cruel taskmaster of the soul, robbing us of our hope and joy. It turns our focus inward, pulling a dark curtain over our eyes so we can't see God's love for us. Even the psalmist cried out in complaint to the Lord, *"You have taken my companions and loved ones from me; darkness is my closest friend"* (Psalm 88:18).

But God desires to break through the dark clouds and restore our sense of purpose in life. He wants to deliver us from our loneliness so we can reach out to others again and fulfill our destiny. If we are living *"solitary"* lives, He wants to give us friends and family to connect with (Psalm 68:6).

Many Biblical heroes experienced feelings of rejection and loneliness, but during such times they drew near to God and discovered that He's *"a friend who sticks closer than a brother"* (Proverbs 18:24).

Let your conduct be without covetousness; be content with such things as you have. For He Himself has said, "I will never leave you nor forsake you."
HEBREWS 13:5

The LORD will not forsake His people, for His great name's sake, because it has pleased the LORD to make you His people.
1 SAMUEL 12:22

LORD, You have been our dwelling place in all generations. Before the mountains were brought forth, or ever You had formed the earth and the world, even from everlasting to everlasting, You are God.
PSALM 90:1-2

Fear not, for I am with you; be not dismayed, for I am your God. I will strengthen you, yes, I will help you, I will uphold you with My righteous right hand.
ISAIAH 41:10

God sets the solitary in families; He brings out those who are bound into prosperity; but the rebellious dwell in a dry land.
PSALM 68:6

When my father and my mother forsake me, then the LORD will take care of me.
PSALM 27:10

I will not leave you orphans; I will come to you.
JOHN 14:18

LONELY

I am persuaded that neither death nor life, nor angels nor principalities nor powers, nor things present nor things to come, nor height nor depth, nor any other created thing, shall be able to separate us from the love of God which is in Christ Jesus our Lord.

ROMANS 8:38-39

"The mountains shall depart and the hills be removed, but My kindness shall not depart from you, nor shall My covenant of peace be removed," says the LORD, who has mercy on you.

ISAIAH 54:10

God is our refuge and strength, a very present help in trouble.

PSALM 46:1

Where can I go from Your Spirit? Or where can I flee from Your presence? If I ascend into heaven, You are there; if I make my bed in hell, behold, You are there. If I take the wings of the morning, and dwell in the uttermost parts of the sea, even there Your hand shall lead me, and Your right hand shall hold me. If I say, "Surely the darkness shall fall on me," even the night shall be light about me; indeed, the darkness shall not hide from You, but the night shines as the day; the darkness and the light are both alike to You.

PSALM 139:7-12

Lo, I am with you always, even to the end of the age.

MATTHEW 28:20

PRAYER

FATHER, *thank You for Your faithfulness to be with me always, even in the dark times when I struggle to feel Your presence. Nothing in Heaven or on earth can separate me from Your love!*

Forgive me for putting my eyes on myself instead of on Your love or the needs of others. Fill me with Your love and help me to reach out again to those around me.

Father, I call on You to heal my heart of wounds or disappointments from any broken relationships. Give me Godly friends and companions to walk with during my journey through life.

In Jesus' name. **AMEN.**

GOD'S PROMISES
for
WHEN YOU NEED REASSURANCE ABOUT...

*Y*OUR CHILDREN

THE BIBLE calls children *"a heritage from the Lord"* and *"a reward"* from Him (Psalm 127:3). But because we love our children and grandchildren so much, it can be very painful when they stray from the Lord.

Thankfully, the Bible is full of promises for parents and grandparents who cry out to God on behalf of their children and grandchildren. Just as with the Prodigal Son (Luke 15), our loved ones may journey to *"a far country."* But like the Prodigal, they can come to their senses and return to the Lord…and to us!

Cry out to God on behalf of your kids and grandkids. And don't give up until you receive the breakthrough you seek!

Believe on the Lord Jesus Christ, and you will be saved, you and your household.

ACTS 16:31

Choose for yourselves this day whom you will serve… But as for me and my house, we will serve the LORD.

JOSHUA 24:15

Train up a child in the way he should go, and when he is old he will not depart from it.

PROVERBS 22:6

Honor your father and your mother, that your days may be long upon the land which the LORD your God is giving you.

EXODUS 20:12

Fathers, do not provoke your children to wrath, but bring them up in the training and admonition of the Lord.

EPHESIANS 6:4

Children are a heritage from the LORD, the fruit of the womb is a reward. Like arrows in the hand of a warrior, so are the children of one's youth. Happy is the man who has his quiver full of them; they shall not be ashamed, but shall speak with their enemies in the gate.

PSALM 127:3-5

He will turn the hearts of the fathers to the children, and the hearts of the children to their fathers, lest I come and strike the earth with a curse.

MALACHI 4:6

Lift up your eyes all around, and see: They all gather together, they come to you; your sons shall come from afar, and your daughters shall be nursed at your side.

ISAIAH 60:4

These words which I command you today shall be in your heart. You shall teach them diligently to your children, and shall talk of them when you sit in your house, when you walk by the way, when you lie down, and when you rise up. You shall bind them as a sign on your hand, and they shall be as frontlets between your eyes. You shall write them on the doorposts of your house and on your gates.

DEUTERONOMY 6:6-9

Blessed is every one who fears the LORD, who walks in His ways. When you eat the labor of your hands, you shall be happy, and it shall be well with you. Your wife shall be like a fruitful vine in the very heart of your house, your children like olive plants all around your table. Behold, thus shall the man be blessed who fears the LORD.

PSALM 128:1-4

Enlarge the place of your tent, and let them stretch out the curtains of your dwellings...For you shall expand to the right and to the left, and your descendants will inherit the nations, and make the desolate cities inhabited.

ISAIAH 54:2-3

PRAYER

HEAVENLY FATHER, *thank You that I can trust my children or grandchildren to You. No matter how far they stray from Your purposes, Your eyes are always on them. They never can outrun Your grace or Your presence!*

Show me specific Scriptures to pray on their behalf. Send them the people and situations they need to help them come to their senses and see Your great calling for their life. May Your Spirit convict them of sin, reveal what Jesus did for them on the Cross, and powerfully draw them back to You.

Thank You, Father, that I can rest in the knowledge that You love them even more than I do. Thank You for setting a hedge of protection around them until they're restored in their relationship with You.

In Jesus' name. **AMEN.**

The silver-haired head is a crown of glory,
if it is found in the way of righteousness.

PROVERBS 16:31

YOUR ELDERLY LOVED ONES

WHEN WE FACE the needs of elderly loved ones, we're often entering uncharted territory—responsibilities and challenges we've never encountered before. While this can be lonely and overwhelming at times, the Lord has promised to be with us and sustain us.

Although it's important to plan ahead for the future needs of your elderly loved ones, remember that God will give you special grace for *each day*. Remember these words of Jesus: *"Therefore do not worry about tomorrow, for tomorrow will worry about its own things. Sufficient for the day is its own trouble"* (Matthew 6:24).

God will never send you a situation too big for you to handle with His help! Whenever you're tempted to feel overwhelmed, meditate on His precious promise: *"My grace is sufficient for you, for My strength is made perfect in weakness"* (2 Corinthians 12:9).

It shall come to pass afterward that I will pour out My Spirit on all flesh; your sons and your daughters shall prophesy, your old men shall dream dreams, your young men shall see visions.

JOEL 2:28

O God, You have taught me from my youth; and to this day I declare Your wondrous works. Now also when I am old and grayheaded, O God, do not forsake me, until I declare Your strength to this generation, Your power to everyone who is to come.

PSALM 71:17-18

Blessed be the LORD, who has not left you this day without a close relative… And may he be to you a restorer of life and a nourisher of your old age.

RUTH 4:14-15

Let your heart keep my commands; for length of days and long life and peace they will add to you.

PROVERBS 3:1-2

With long life I will satisfy him, and show him My salvation.

PSALM 91:16

I have been young, and now am old; yet I have not seen the righteous forsaken, nor his descendants begging bread.

PSALM 37:25

Yea, though I walk through the valley of the shadow of death, I will fear no evil; for You are with me; Your rod and Your staff, they comfort me.

PSALM 23:4

The LORD blessed the latter days of Job more than his beginning.
JOB 42:12

Pure and undefiled religion before God and the Father is this: to visit orphans and widows in their trouble, and to keep oneself unspotted from the world.
JAMES 1:27

Even to your old age, I am He, and even to gray hairs I will carry you! I have made, and I will bear; even I will carry, and will deliver you.
ISAIAH 46:4

David, after he had served his own generation by the will of God, fell asleep.
ACTS 13:36

Surely goodness and mercy shall follow me all the days of my life; and I will dwell in the house of the LORD forever.
PSALM 23:6

Those who are planted in the house of the LORD shall flourish in the courts of our God. They shall still bear fruit in old age; they shall be fresh and flourishing, to declare that the LORD is upright; He is my rock, and there is no unrighteousness in Him.
PSALM 92:13-15

You shall go to your fathers in peace; you shall be buried at a good old age.
GENESIS 15:15

PRAYER

HEAVENLY FATHER, *I trust You to give me the grace I need for the challenges of each day. Help me to keep me eyes on Your faithful provision instead of on the difficult burdens I face.*

Thank You that I can rest secure in Your great compassion and care for my loved ones. Give me wisdom to know what my role should be in their lives.

Father, I pray You would powerfully minister to my elderly loved ones with Your healing and comforting presence. Draw them close to You and give them assurance of eternal life through Your Son Jesus.

In Jesus' name. **AMEN.**

The Spirit Himself bears witness with our spirit that we are children of God.

ROMANS 8:16

ETERNAL LIFE

MANY PEOPLE are uncertain about where they stand with God and whether they will be with Him when they die. Often this is because they're basing their salvation on their own merit and good deeds, rather than on the merit of Jesus' death on the Cross.

If you've given your life to Christ, the Bible makes it clear He wants to give you full assurance that you have eternal life: *"He who has the Son has life; he who does not have the Son of God does not have life. These things I have written to you who believe in the name of the Son of God, that you may know that you have eternal life"* (1 John 5:12-13).

Do you have assurance that you will spend eternity with the Lord when you leave this life? If not, take time to pray the Salvation Prayer on pages 235-236. And ask Him for assurance of your salvation today as you read these promises from His Word.

This is the testimony: that God has given us eternal life, and this life is in His Son.

1 JOHN 5:11

Most assuredly, I say to you, he who hears My word and believes in Him who sent Me has everlasting life, and shall not come into judgment, but has passed from death into life.

JOHN 5:24

Surely goodness and mercy shall follow me all the days of my life; and I will dwell in the house of the LORD forever.

PSALM 23:6

The wages of sin is death, but the gift of God is eternal life in Christ Jesus our Lord.

ROMANS 6:23

This is eternal life, that they may know You, the only true God, and Jesus Christ whom You have sent.

JOHN 17:3

Do not labor for the food which perishes, but for the food which endures to everlasting life, which the Son of Man will give you.

JOHN 6:27

God so loved the world that He gave His only begotten Son, that whoever believes in Him should not perish but have everlasting life.

JOHN 3:16

Fight the good fight of faith, lay hold on eternal life, to which you were also called.

1 TIMOTHY 6:12

We know that the Son of God has come and has given us an understanding, that we may know Him who is true; and we are in Him who is true, in His Son Jesus Christ. This is the true God and eternal life.

1 JOHN 5:20

My sheep hear My voice, and I know them, and they follow Me. And I give them eternal life, and they shall never perish; neither shall anyone snatch them out of My hand.

JOHN 10:27-28

I am the resurrection and the life. He who believes in Me, though he may die, he shall live. And whoever lives and believes in Me shall never die.

JOHN 11:25-26

God will redeem my soul from the power of the grave, for He shall receive me.

PSALM 49:15

When this corruptible has put on incorruption, and this mortal has put on immortality, then shall be brought to pass the saying that is written: "Death is swallowed up in victory." "O Death, where is your sting? O Hades, where is your victory?"

1 CORINTHIANS 15:54-55

These things I have written to you who believe in the name of the Son of God, that you may know that you have eternal life, and that you may continue to believe in the name of the Son of God.

1 JOHN 5:13

PRAYER

FATHER, *thank You that I can know for sure You've given me eternal life. I ask You to give me this deep assurance today, not based on my own efforts but by faith in what You did in sending Your Son to die in my place.*

May Your Holy Spirit give me an inner peace today, testifying that I am indeed Your beloved child, destined to live with You for eternity. And thank You that I can know You now, even in this life!

Father, give me an eternal perspective on my life, and help me align my time, talent, and treasure with Your Kingdom.

In Jesus' name. **AMEN.**

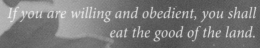

If you are willing and obedient, you shall eat the good of the land.

ISAIAH 1:19

GOD'S BLESSINGS FOR OBEDIENCE

TO MANY PEOPLE, God seems to allocate His blessings in a totally random way. But the Bible says our choices and actions have a major role to play in the blessings and rewards we receive from the Lord. Deuteronomy 28 and other passages list the blessings of obedience to God and the curses upon disobedience. The contrast is *huge*!

Today God sets an important decision before you: *"I have set before you life and death, blessing and cursing; therefore choose life, that both you and your descendants may live; that you may love the LORD your God, that you may obey His voice, and that you may cling to Him, for He is your life and the length of your days"* (Deuteronomy 30:19-20).

Choose *life* today! Choose to obey the Lord, and watch Him bless you!

Obey My voice, and I will be your God, and you shall be My people. And walk in all the ways that I have commanded you, that it may be well with you.

JEREMIAH 7:23

If you love Me, keep My commandments. He who has My commandments and keeps them, it is he who loves Me. And he who loves Me will be loved by My Father, and I will love him and manifest Myself to him.

JOHN 14:15, 21

Oh, that you had heeded My commandments! Then your peace would have been like a river, and your righteousness like the waves of the sea.

ISAIAH 48:18

Behold, I set before you today a blessing and a curse: the blessing, if you obey the commandments of the LORD your God which I command you today; and the curse, if you do not obey the commandments of the LORD your God, but turn aside from the way which I command you today, to go after other gods which you have not known.

DEUTERONOMY 11:26-28

Whoever keeps His word, truly the love of God is perfected in him. By this we know that we are in Him. He who says he abides in Him ought himself also to walk just as He walked.

1 JOHN 2:5-6

You shall keep every commandment which I command you today, that you may be strong, and go in and possess the land which you cross over to possess, and that you may prolong your days in the land which the LORD swore to give your fathers, to them and their descendants, "a land flowing with milk and honey…." And it shall be that if you earnestly obey My commandments which I command you today, to love the LORD your God and serve Him with all your heart and with all your soul, then I will give you the rain for your land in its season, the early rain and the latter rain, that you may gather in your grain, your new wine, and your oil. And I will send grass in your fields for your livestock, that you may eat and be filled…Every place on which the sole of your foot treads shall be yours… For you will cross over the Jordan and go in to possess the land which the LORD your God is giving you, and you will possess it and dwell in it.

DEUTERONOMY 11:8-31

If you walk in My ways, to keep My statutes and My commandments, as your father David walked, then I will lengthen your days.

1 KINGS 3:14

Teach me to do Your will, for You are my God; Your Spirit is good. Lead me in the land of uprightness.

PSALM 143:10

PRAYER

HEAVENLY FATHER, *I choose to obey You. I trust Your plan for my life. Teach me more of Your Word and let me hear Your voice more clearly.*

Thank You for the abundant life You've prepared for me. I want to walk in Your ways and serve Your purposes in my generation. I want to leave a Godly heritage to my loved ones. And I want to impact lives for eternity!

Father, may this day mark a new beginning of obedience and blessings in my life. Thank You for Your great promises!

In Jesus' name. **AMEN.**

GOD'S FAITHFULNESS

PEOPLE WILL INEVITABLY let us down from time to time. The psalmist said in alarm, *"All men are liars"* (Psalm 116:11), and King Solomon asked, *"Who can find a faithful man?"* (Proverbs 20:6).

But the good news is that while people may be unfaithful, God is *always* faithful! You can put your trust fully in Him and in the promises of His Word.

That's why the psalmist declared, *"Forever, O* Lord, *Your word is settled in heaven"* (Psalm 119:89). You can be confident that if the Bible says something, that *settles* the matter!

This I recall to my mind, therefore I have hope. Through the LORD's mercies we are not consumed, because His compassions fail not. They are new every morning; great is Your faithfulness. "The LORD is my portion," says my soul, "Therefore I hope in Him!"

LAMENTATIONS 3:21-24

"For the mountains shall depart and the hills be removed, but My kindness shall not depart from you, nor shall My covenant of peace be removed," says the LORD, who has mercy on you.

ISAIAH 54:10

He who calls you is faithful, who also will do it.

1 THESSALONIANS 5:24

Behold, I am with you and will keep you wherever you go, and will bring you back to this land; for I will not leave you until I have done what I have spoken to you.

GENESIS 28:15

He is God, the faithful God who keeps covenant and mercy for a thousand generations with those who love Him and keep His commandments.

DEUTERONOMY 7:9

Not one thing has failed of all the good things which the LORD your God spoke concerning you. All have come to pass for you; not one word of them has failed.

JOSHUA 23:14

GOD'S FAITHFULNESS

I will sing of the mercies of the LORD forever; with my mouth will I make known Your faithfulness to all generations. For I have said, "Mercy shall be built up forever; Your faithfulness You shall establish in the very heavens."
PSALM 89:1-2

No temptation has overtaken you except such as is common to man; but God is faithful, who will not allow you to be tempted beyond what you are able, but with the temptation will also make the way of escape, that you may be able to bear it.
1 CORINTHIANS 10:13

Your testimonies, which You have commanded, are righteous and very faithful.
PSALM 119:138

If we are faithless, He remains faithful; He cannot deny Himself.
2 TIMOTHY 2:13

He will not allow your foot to be moved; He who keeps you will not slumber. Behold, He who keeps Israel shall neither slumber nor sleep.
PSALM 121:3-4

Trust in the LORD, and do good; dwell in the land, and feed on His faithfulness. Delight yourself also in the LORD, and He shall give you the desires of your heart.
PSALM 37:3-4

Your faithfulness endures to all generations.
PSALM 119:90

PRAYER

LORD, *You are my faithful Rock in the midst of life's storms.*
Not one of Your promises has ever failed!

Thank You, Lord, for speaking to me through Your Scriptures.
I choose to believe and claim Your great promises for my life,
knowing that Your Word is forever settled in Heaven.

May my life reflect Your faithfulness.
I put my hope and confidence in You!

In Jesus' name. **AMEN.**

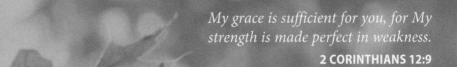

My grace is sufficient for you, for My strength is made perfect in weakness.

2 CORINTHIANS 12:9

GOD'S GRACE

EVERY BLESSING we receive in life is a gift of God's grace. Instead of bringing us into judgment and condemnation, He offers us grace and mercy through Jesus' death for us on the Cross.

The Bible says God's grace is both our entryway into salvation and also our empowerment to live the Christian life. Through grace we are accepted by God, and it's by grace that we have strength to overcome the many challenges we face in this world.

Remember as you read these verses that God doesn't give you His grace because you *deserve* it, but rather because of the *unmerited favor* He has shown to you in Christ.

By grace you have been saved through faith, and that not of yourselves; it is the gift of God, not of works, lest anyone should boast. For we are His workmanship, created in Christ Jesus for good works, which God prepared beforehand that we should walk in them.

EPHESIANS 2:8-10

We ourselves were also once foolish, disobedient, deceived, serving various lusts and pleasures, living in malice and envy, hateful and hating one another. But when the kindness and the love of God our Savior toward man appeared, not by works of righteousness which we have done, but according to His mercy He saved us, through the washing of regeneration and renewing of the Holy Spirit, whom He poured out on us abundantly through Jesus Christ our Savior, that having been justified by His grace we should become heirs according to the hope of eternal life.

TITUS 3:3-7

The grace of God that brings salvation has appeared to all men, teaching us that, denying ungodliness and worldly lusts, we should live soberly, righteously, and godly in the present age, looking for the blessed hope and glorious appearing of our great God and Savior Jesus Christ, who gave Himself for us, that He might redeem us from every lawless deed and purify for Himself His own special people, zealous for good works.

TITUS 2:11-14

To the praise of the glory of His grace, by which He made us accepted in the Beloved.

EPHESIANS 1:6

Of His fullness we have all received, and grace for grace. For the law was given through Moses, but grace and truth came through Jesus Christ.

JOHN 1:16-17

Let us therefore come boldly to the throne of grace, that we may obtain mercy and find grace to help in time of need.

HEBREWS 4:16

You have found grace in My sight, and I know you by name.

EXODUS 33:17

With great power the apostles gave witness to the resurrection of the Lord Jesus. And great grace was upon them all.

ACTS 4:33

By the grace of God I am what I am, and His grace toward me was not in vain; but I labored more abundantly than they all, yet not I, but the grace of God which was with me.

1 CORINTHIANS 15:10

You know the grace of our Lord Jesus Christ, that though He was rich, yet for your sakes He became poor, that you through His poverty might become rich.

2 CORINTHIANS 8:9

PRAYER

HEAVENLY FATHER, *I'm so grateful for Your grace!*
Through Jesus, You paid the debt of my sin and brought me into
right standing with You. You took my sickness, poverty, and death
and gave me Your health, prosperity, and eternal life instead.

Father, I come boldly to Your throne of grace today to receive the
provision and breakthroughs I need from You. Thank You
that I can approach You without fear or condemnation!

May Your grace continue to transform my life
and shape me into the image of Your Son Jesus!

In Jesus' name. **AMEN.**

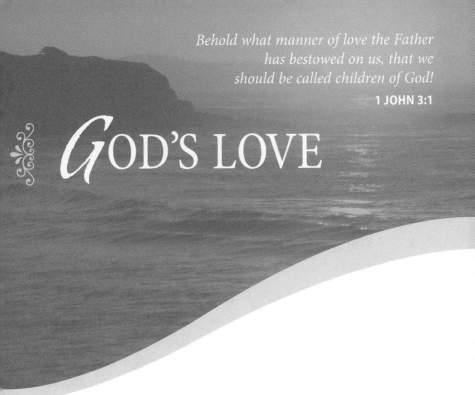

Behold what manner of love the Father has bestowed on us, that we should be called children of God!

1 JOHN 3:1

*G*OD'S LOVE

MOST HUMAN LOVE is conditional, based on the conduct, response, or perceived worthiness of the recipient. That's why it's so easy to love our friends, but not our enemies.

In contrast, the Bible points to the Lord's amazing unconditional love: "*God demonstrates His own love toward us, in that while we were still sinners, Christ died for us*" (Romans 5:8). Instead of waiting until we were more deserving, God chose to love us when we were still sinners—when we were His enemies!

You don't need to be in doubt about God's love for you today. He sent His Son to die in your place, even before you did anything to deserve it!

Beloved, let us love one another, for love is of God; and everyone who loves is born of God and knows God. He who does not love does not know God, for God is love.

1 John 4:7-8

Love suffers long and is kind; love does not envy; love does not parade itself, is not puffed up; does not behave rudely, does not seek its own, is not provoked, thinks no evil; does not rejoice in iniquity, but rejoices in the truth; bears all things, believes all things, hopes all things, endures all things. Love never fails. But whether there are prophecies, they will fail; whether there are tongues, they will cease; whether there is knowledge, it will vanish away.

1 Corinthians 13:4-8

In this is love, not that we loved God, but that He loved us and sent His Son to be the propitiation for our sins. Beloved, if God so loved us, we also ought to love one another.

1 John 4:10-11

As the Father loved Me, I also have loved you; abide in My love. If you keep My commandments, you will abide in My love, just as I have kept My Father's commandments and abide in His love.

John 15:9-10

Greater love has no one than this, than to lay down one's life for his friends.

John 15:13

I am persuaded that neither death nor life, nor angels nor principalities nor powers, nor things present nor things to come, nor height nor depth, nor any other created thing, shall be able to separate us from the love of God which is in Christ Jesus our Lord.

ROMANS 8:38-39

God, who is rich in mercy, because of His great love with which He loved us, even when we were dead in trespasses, made us alive together with Christ (by grace you have been saved), and raised us up together, and made us sit together in the heavenly places in Christ Jesus, that in the ages to come He might show the exceeding riches of His grace in His kindness toward us in Christ Jesus.

EPHESIANS 2:4-7

Yes, I have loved you with an everlasting love; therefore with lovingkindness I have drawn you.

JEREMIAH 31:3

God so loved the world that He gave His only begotten Son, that whoever believes in Him should not perish but have everlasting life.

JOHN 3:16

A new commandment I give to you, that you love one another; as I have loved you, that you also love one another. By this all will know that you are My disciples, if you have love for one another.

JOHN 13:34-35

PRAYER

HEAVENLY FATHER, *I'm grateful that You not only have declared Your love, but You've also demonstrated it. Thank You for showing Your great love for me before I did anything at all to deserve it!*

You are the only reliable Source of love, and I draw on that supply so I can show love to others. May Your love flow through me to everyone I meet.

Thank You, Father, that nothing can separate me from the love You've given me in Your Son. Thank You that You will wrap Your loving arms around me for all eternity!

In Jesus' name. **AMEN.**

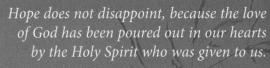

Hope does not disappoint, because the love of God has been poured out in our hearts by the Holy Spirit who was given to us.

ROMANS 5:5

THE HOLY SPIRIT

FOR MANY PEOPLE, the Holy Spirit is a mysterious or even scary force. Yet the Bible says God exists as the Father, Jesus, and the Holy Spirit—and these three are one.

No one can possibly live the Christian life apart from the empowerment of God's Spirit. He convicts us of sin, reveals Jesus to us and through us, and empowers us to be witnesses to a lost and needy world.

God wants to FILL you with His Spirit. Then you will have greater intimacy with Him (John 15:26), boldness to speak His Word (Acts 4:31), and the spiritual fruit of Christ-like character (Galatians 5:22-23). As you read these verses, be filled with the Holy Spirit!

I will pray the Father, and He will give you another Helper, that He may abide with you forever—the Spirit of truth, whom the world cannot receive, because it neither sees Him nor knows Him; but you know Him, for He dwells with you and will be in you.

JOHN 14:16-17

I will give you a new heart and put a new spirit within you; I will take the heart of stone out of your flesh and give you a heart of flesh. I will put My Spirit within you and cause you to walk in My statutes, and you will keep My judgments and do them.

EZEKIEL 36:26-27

Do not be drunk with wine, in which is dissipation; but be filled with the Spirit.

EPHESIANS 5:18

When He, the Spirit of truth, has come, He will guide you into all truth; for He will not speak on His own authority, but whatever He hears He will speak; and He will tell you things to come.

JOHN 16:13

It shall come to pass afterward that I will pour out My Spirit on all flesh; your sons and your daughters shall prophesy, your old men shall dream dreams, your young men shall see visions.

JOEL 2:28

Do you not know that your body is the temple of the Holy Spirit who is in you, whom you have from God, and you are not your own?

1 CORINTHIANS 6:19

THE HOLY SPIRIT

You shall receive power when the Holy Spirit has come upon you; and you shall be witnesses to Me in Jerusalem, and in all Judea and Samaria, and to the end of the earth.

ACTS 1:8

"He who believes in Me, as the Scripture has said, out of his heart will flow rivers of living water." But this He spoke concerning the Spirit, whom those believing in Him would receive; for the Holy Spirit was not yet given, because Jesus was not yet glorified.

JOHN 7:38-39

They were all filled with the Holy Spirit and began to speak with other tongues, as the Spirit gave them utterance.

ACTS 2:4

The fruit of the Spirit is love, joy, peace, longsuffering, kindness, goodness, faithfulness, gentleness, self-control.

GALATIANS 5:22-23

Repent, and let every one of you be baptized in the name of Jesus Christ for the remission of sins; and you shall receive the gift of the Holy Spirit.

ACTS 2:38

When they had prayed, the place where they were assembled together was shaken; and they were all filled with the Holy Spirit, and they spoke the word of God with boldness.

ACTS 4:31

PRAYER

HOLY SPIRIT, *I empty my heart and ask You
to come and fill me to overflowing with Your life and power.
Renew me, strengthen me, and restore my joy.*

*Empower me to glorify Jesus in my life and be a bold witness for
Him. I submit to You in gratitude for Your great promise to
fill my life with love, joy, peace, longsuffering, kindness, goodness,
faithfulness, gentleness, and self-control.*

*I surrender my body for You to use as Your holy temple,
and I pray that rivers of life-giving water will flow from
my life to my loved ones and a lost and needy world.*

In Jesus' name. **AMEN.**

UNSAVED LOVED ONES

DID YOU KNOW that God cares even more about your unsaved loved ones than you do? The Bible makes it clear that He *"desires **all** men to be saved and to come to the knowledge of the truth"* (1 Timothy 2:4).

Take a few minutes right now and pray this verse on behalf of your loved ones who don't know the Lord yet: "Father, thank You that You desire [insert your loved one's name] to be saved and to come to the knowledge of the truth."

What a joy it is to align your prayers with what God has already declared as His will! Pray in faith, trusting the Lord to draw your loved ones to Himself.

So they said, "Believe on the Lord Jesus Christ, and you will be saved, you and your household." Then they spoke the word of the Lord to him and to all who were in his house. And he took them the same hour of the night and washed their stripes. And immediately he and all his family were baptized. Now when he had brought them into his house, he set food before them; and he rejoiced, having believed in God with all his household.

ACTS 16:31-34

Those who sow in tears shall reap in joy. He who continually goes forth weeping, bearing seed for sowing, shall doubtless come again with rejoicing, bringing his sheaves with him.

PSALM 126:5-6

The Lord is not slack concerning His promise, as some count slackness, but is longsuffering toward us, not willing that any should perish but that all should come to repentance.

2 PETER 3:9

God did not send His Son into the world to condemn the world, but that the world through Him might be saved.

JOHN 3:17

The Son of Man has come to seek and to save that which was lost.

LUKE 19:10

Most assuredly, I say to you, unless one is born again, he cannot see the kingdom of God.

JOHN 3:3

UNSAVED LOVED ONES

There will be more joy in heaven over one sinner who repents than over ninety-nine just persons who need no repentance.

LUKE 15:7

Come to Me, all you who labor and are heavy laden, and I will give you rest. Take My yoke upon you and learn from Me, for I am gentle and lowly in heart, and you will find rest for your souls. For My yoke is easy and My burden is light.

MATTHEW 11:28-30

Restore to me the joy of Your salvation, and uphold me by Your generous Spirit. Then I will teach transgressors Your ways, and sinners shall be converted to You.

PSALM 51:12-13

[The prodigal son] arose and came to his father. But when he was still a great way off, his father saw him and had compassion, and ran and fell on his neck and kissed him. And the son said to him, "Father, I have sinned against heaven and in your sight, and am no longer worthy to be called your son." But the father said to his servants, "Bring out the best robe and put it on him, and put a ring on his hand and sandals on his feet. And bring the fatted calf here and kill it, and let us eat and be merry…It was right that we should make merry and be glad, for your brother was dead and is alive again, and was lost and is found."

LUKE 15:20-32

PRAYER

HEAVENLY FATHER, *thank You for assuring me of Your desire to see my loved ones saved. I pray in faith today, joining my prayer to the truth of Your Word. I release my loved ones into Your mighty hands, asking You to draw them by Your Spirit.*

Lord, may You open their eyes to Your love. Show them what Jesus did for them on the Cross. I rebuke every scheme of the enemy to deceive them and blind their eyes!

I thank You in advance for the great celebration that will happen in Heaven when my loved ones fully give their lives to You!

In Jesus' name. **AMEN.**

GOD'S PROMISES
for
WHEN YOU'RE STRUGGLING WITH...

ᴀDDICTION

IF YOU OR A LOVED ONE find yourselves bound by a sinful habit or addiction today, Jesus wants to set you free. The Bible teaches that *"whoever commits sin is a slave of sin,"* but His Word also promises liberation to all who commit their lives fully to Him: *"If the Son sets you free, you shall be free indeed"* (John 8:34-36).

John 11 tells the story of Jesus raising His friend Lazarus from the dead. Even after Lazarus was brought back to life, he still was tightly wrapped with grave clothes. Does that describe you or a loved one today? Has Christ given you new life, yet you find yourself still bound by stinky "grave clothes" from your prior sinful life?

Jesus said to those around Lazarus: *"Loose him, and let him go!"* In the same way, Jesus wants to unwrap your grave clothes and set you free to live a victorious and abundant life in Him!

YOUR PROMISES *from* GOD'S WORD

Let us search out and
examine our ways, and
turn back to the LORD.

LAMENTATIONS 3:40

Confess your trespasses to
one another, and pray for
one another, that you may
be healed.

JAMES 5:16

I know that in me (that is,
in my flesh) nothing good
dwells; for to will is present
with me, but how to
perform what is good I do
not find…O wretched man
that I am! Who will deliver
me from this body of death?
I thank God—through Jesus
Christ our Lord!

ROMANS 7:18, 24-25

My grace is sufficient for
you, for My strength is made
perfect in weakness.

2 CORINTHIANS 12:9

It is God who works in you
both to will and to do for
His good pleasure.

PHILIPPIANS 2:13

I have been crucified with
Christ; it is no longer I who
live, but Christ lives in me;
and the life which I now live
in the flesh I live by faith in
the Son of God, who loved
me and gave Himself for me.

GALATIANS 2:20

Search me, O God, and
know my heart; try me, and
know my anxieties; and see
if there is any wicked way in
me, and lead me in the way
everlasting.

PSALM 139:23-24

The Lord is faithful, who will establish you and guard you from the evil one.

2 THESSALONIANS 3:3

Humble yourselves in the sight of the Lord, and He will lift you up.

JAMES 4:10

There is therefore now no condemnation to those who are in Christ Jesus…For the law of the Spirit of life in Christ Jesus has made me free from the law of sin and death. For what the law could not do in that it was weak through the flesh, God did by sending His own Son…that the righteous requirement of the law might be fulfilled in us who do not walk according to the flesh but according to the Spirit.

ROMANS 8:1-4

Let the words of my mouth and the meditation of my heart be acceptable in Your sight, O LORD, my strength and my Redeemer.

PSALM 19:14

Brethren, if a man is overtaken in any trespass, you who are spiritual restore such a one in a spirit of gentleness, considering yourself lest you also be tempted. Bear one another's burdens, and so fulfill the law of Christ.

GALATIANS 6:1-2

Most assuredly, I say to you, whoever commits sin is a slave of sin.

JOHN 8:34

PRAYER

LORD JESUS, *thank You for Your desire to set me free and give me an abundant life in You. Show me Your truth, and open up the door to my freedom from sinful habits and addictions.*

Lord, I ask You to reveal the root causes for any bondage in my life. I submit to You and stand against the devil's lies. I break Satan's power by the blood You shed for me on the Cross.

Thank You for healing any inner wounds that make me vulnerable to Satan's schemes, Lord. I forgive anyone who has wronged me, just as You have graciously forgiven me. Thank You for this new day of healing, hope, freedom, and victory in my life!

In Your name. **AMEN.**

Submit to God.
Resist the devil and he will flee from you.
JAMES 4:7

THE DEVIL

THE BIBLE SAYS God's people are engaged in an epic battle against the forces of darkness (Ephesians 6:10-12). This battle is largely unseen, waged in the spiritual realm. But whether you realize it or not, you are being affected by this spiritual battle as you seek to grow in the Lord and break away from any stronghold the devil has had in your life.

The good news is that God offers us all the spiritual weapons and armor we need for victory! Instead of being defenseless victims, the Bible says *"we are more than conquerors through Him who loved us"* (Romans 8:37).

We have a very real spiritual adversary, and he comes as a thief *"to steal, and to kill, and to destroy"* (John 10:10). Yet when we put our trust in the Lord, we can say with the apostle Paul: *"Thanks be to God who always leads us in triumph in Christ"* (2 Corinthians 2:14).

My brethren, be strong in the Lord and in the power of His might. Put on the whole armor of God, that you may be able to stand against the wiles of the devil. For we do not wrestle against flesh and blood, but against principalities, against powers, against the rulers of the darkness of this age, against spiritual hosts of wickedness in the heavenly places.

Therefore take up the whole armor of God, that you may be able to withstand in the evil day, and having done all, to stand. Stand therefore, having girded your waist with truth, having put on the breastplate of righteousness, and having shod your feet with the preparation of the gospel of peace; above all, taking the shield of faith with which you will be able to quench all the fiery darts of the wicked one.

And take the helmet of salvation, and the sword of the Spirit, which is the word of God; praying always with all prayer and supplication in the Spirit, being watchful to this end with all perseverance and supplication for all the saints.

EPHESIANS 6:10-18

For this purpose the Son of God was manifested, that He might destroy the works of the devil.

1 JOHN 3:8

If God is for us, who can be against us?

ROMANS 8:31

You have been a shelter for me, a strong tower from the enemy.

PSALM 61:3

Then the seventy returned with joy, saying, "Lord, even the demons are subject to us in Your name." And He said to them, "I saw Satan fall like lightning from heaven. Behold, I give you the authority to trample on serpents and scorpions, and over all the power of the enemy, and nothing shall by any means hurt you."

LUKE 10:17-19

Having disarmed principalities and powers, He made a public spectacle of them, triumphing over them in [the Cross].

COLOSSIANS 2:15

Deliver us from the evil one. For Yours is the kingdom and the power and the glory forever.

MATTHEW 6:13

Be sober, be vigilant; because your adversary the devil walks about like a roaring lion, seeking whom he may devour. Resist him, steadfast in the faith, knowing that the same sufferings are experienced by your brotherhood in the world.

1 PETER 5:8-9

They overcame [Satan, the accuser] by the blood of the Lamb and by the word of their testimony, and they did not love their lives to the death.

REVELATION 12:11

You are of God, little children, and have overcome them, because He who is in you is greater than he who is in the world.

1 JOHN 4:4

PRAYER

HEAVENLY FATHER, *thank You for giving me Your powerful spiritual weapons to defeat the enemy. Train me for battle, and give me boldness to go on the offensive against Satan's strongholds.*

Today I put on Your spiritual armor to cover every part of me from the fiery darts of Satan's unseen army. By the blood Jesus shed for me on the Cross, I break every curse or bondage Satan would try to put on me or my loved ones. Submitting my life fully to God, I resist the devil, and he must flee from me!

Lord, I ask You to live big within me today by the power of the Holy Spirit. Instead of cowering in fear, I will rise up to claim my inheritance and destiny in You!

In Jesus' name. **AMEN.**

> *He heals the brokenhearted*
> *and binds up their wounds.*
>
> **PSALM 147:3**

DIVORCE

FEW EXPERIENCES in life are as painful as the sting of divorce. Regardless of the causes or circumstances that led to that sad outcome, divorce usually brings feelings of rejection, betrayal, failure, anger, and confusion.

If you are dealing with the painful reality of divorce today, God wants you to know that He can help you put your life together again. He wants to wrap His loving arms around you, bringing hope and healing to your troubled heart.

In the book of Hosea we see a picture of God's difficult relationship with Israel even to the point of His declaring, *"She is not my wife, and I am not her husband."* Yet even through Israel's *"adultery"* and *"unfaithfulness,"* God offered a *"door of hope"* to bring restoration and healing. Regardless of what you may be going through today, God offers you a door of hope and restoration when you give Him the broken pieces of your life.

Fear not, for I am with you; be not dismayed, for I am your God. I will strengthen you, yes, I will help you, I will uphold you with My righteous right hand.

ISAIAH 41:10

Blessed be the God and Father of our Lord Jesus Christ, the Father of mercies and God of all comfort, who comforts us in all our tribulation, that we may be able to comfort those who are in any trouble, with the comfort with which we ourselves are comforted by God.

2 CORINTHIANS 1:3-4

The LORD God is my strength; He will make my feet like deer's feet, and He will make me walk on my high hills.

HABAKKUK 3:19

The LORD is near to those who have a broken heart.

PSALM 34:18

The Spirit of the Lord GOD is upon Me, because the LORD has anointed Me to preach good tidings to the poor; He has sent Me to heal the brokenhearted, to proclaim liberty to the captives, and the opening of the prison to those who are bound; to proclaim the acceptable year of the LORD, and the day of vengeance of our God; to comfort all who mourn, to console those who mourn in Zion, to give them beauty for ashes, the oil of joy for mourning, the garment of praise for the spirit of heaviness; that they may be called trees of righteousness, the planting of the LORD, that He may be glorified.

ISAIAH 61:1-3

DIVORCE

"For the LORD God of Israel says that He hates divorce, for it covers one's garment with violence," says the LORD of hosts. "Therefore take heed to your spirit, that you do not deal treacherously."
MALACHI 2:16

He Himself has said, "I will never leave you nor forsake you." So we may boldly say: "The Lord is my helper; I will not fear. What can man do to me?"
HEBREWS 13:5-6

Do not cast away your confidence, which has great reward.
HEBREWS 10:35

In all these things we are more than conquerors through Him who loved us.
ROMANS 8:37

The Lord will be your confidence, and will keep your foot from being caught.
PROVERBS 3:26

I am persuaded that neither death nor life, nor angels nor principalities nor powers, nor things present nor things to come, nor height nor depth, nor any other created thing, shall be able to separate us from the love of God which is in Christ Jesus our Lord.
ROMANS 8:38-39

The ransomed of the LORD shall return, and come to Zion with singing, with everlasting joy on their heads. They shall obtain joy and gladness; sorrow and sighing shall flee away.
ISAIAH 51:11

PRAYER

FATHER, *it seems that no one really knows how I'm feeling during this painful time in my life—but YOU do. Lord, I need You to wrap Your strong and caring arms around me, reassuring me of Your never-ending love.*

I give You the broken pieces of my life today, asking You to bring me hope, healing, and restoration. I repent of any wrong choices I've made during this painful journey, and I ask You to forgive me. I also choose to forgive anyone who has wronged me during this time. Despite my pain and anger, I ask You to forgive and restore them too.

Father, thank You for pointing me to a door of hope for my future. I choose to enter Your presence, worship You, and seek Your purposes for my life. Thank You for encouraging my heart and giving me a new beginning.

In Jesus' name. **AMEN.**

$\mathcal{D}$OUBT

ONE DAY Jesus was approached by a man seeking deliverance for his demon-oppressed son. Jesus told him, *"If you can believe, all things are possible to him who believes."* To this the man gave a surprisingly honest reply: *"Lord, I believe; help my unbelief!"* (Mark 9:23-24).

Often we approach the Lord with a combination of faith and unbelief. This double-mindedness certainly undercuts the power of our prayers (James 1:5-8; Mark 11:22-24). Nevertheless, the man in this story received the answer to his request of the Lord.

Even if you sense you don't have "perfect" faith today, bring God the faith you DO have, and He will help you in your unbelief!

Let us lay aside every weight, and the sin which so easily ensnares us, and let us run with endurance the race that is set before us, looking unto Jesus, the author and finisher of our faith.

HEBREWS 12:1-2

Jesus answered and said to them, "Have faith in God. For assuredly, I say to you, whoever says to this mountain, 'Be removed and be cast into the sea,' and does not doubt in his heart, but believes that those things he says will be done, he will have whatever he says. Therefore I say to you, whatever things you ask when you pray, believe that you receive them, and you will have them."

MARK 11:22-24

The apostles said to the Lord, "Increase our faith."

LUKE 17:5

[Abraham] did not waver at the promise of God through unbelief, but was strengthened in faith, giving glory to God, and being fully convinced that what He had promised He was also able to perform.

ROMANS 4:20-21

Without faith it is impossible to please Him, for he who comes to God must believe that He is, and that He is a rewarder of those who diligently seek Him.

HEBREWS 11:6

Weeping may endure for a night, but joy comes in the morning.

PSALM 30:5

DOUBT

If any of you lacks wisdom, let him ask of God, who gives to all liberally and without reproach, and it will be given to him. But let him ask in faith, with no doubting, for he who doubts is like a wave of the sea driven and tossed by the wind. For let not that man suppose that he will receive anything from the Lord; he is a double-minded man, unstable in all his ways.

JAMES 1:5-8

With men it is impossible, but not with God; for with God all things are possible.

MARK 10:27

Abraham believed God, and it was accounted to him for righteousness.

JAMES 2:23

I am not ashamed of the gospel of Christ, for it is the power of God to salvation for everyone who believes, for the Jew first and also for the Greek. For in it the righteousness of God is revealed from faith to faith; as it is written, "The just shall live by faith."

ROMANS 1:16-17

Whatever is not from faith is sin.

ROMANS 14:23

The ransomed of the LORD shall return, and come to Zion with singing, with everlasting joy on their heads. They shall obtain joy and gladness; sorrow and sighing shall flee away.

ISAIAH 51:11

PRAYER

LORD JESUS, *I look to You as the Author
and Finisher of my faith. Although my faith is far from perfect
today, I bring You the "mustard seed" of faith I do have.*

*Help me in my unbelief, Lord. Increase my faith so I can pray
with boldness. May I live for You confidently and expectantly.*

*Forgive my unbelief, and fill me with a new, active, obedient faith.
Thank You for being faithful and worthy of my trust!*

In Your name. **AMEN.**

FORGIVING OTHERS

THE BIBLE presents the matter of forgiving others as a *command* rather than an option! Jesus even warns that those who fail to forgive will be handed over to *"the torturers"* (see Matthew 18:21-35). We may think that by carrying a grudge we are "getting back" at someone who has wronged us, but in reality, we are just opening up our life to torment from the enemy!

Forgiveness is a decision, not a feeling. Jesus also warned that our own experience of forgiveness from God will be blocked when we hold on to unforgiveness toward others.

Perhaps you feel you've been hurt too deeply, and treated too unfairly, to forgive the other person. But remember Jesus' amazing example when He pronounced forgiveness on those who beat Him and nailed Him to the Cross: *"Father, forgive them, for they do not know what they do"* (Luke 23:34).

Love your enemies, bless those who curse you, do good to those who hate you, and pray for those who spitefully use you and persecute you.

MATTHEW 5:44

If you forgive men their trespasses, your heavenly Father will also forgive you. But if you do not forgive men their trespasses, neither will your Father forgive your trespasses.

MATTHEW 6:14-15

Peter came to Him and said, "Lord, how often shall my brother sin against me, and I forgive him? Up to seven times?" Jesus said to him, "I do not say to you, up to seven times, but up to seventy times seven."

MATTHEW 18:21-22

Take heed to yourselves. If your brother sins against you, rebuke him; and if he repents, forgive him.

LUKE 17:3

Whenever you stand praying, if you have anything against anyone, forgive him, that your Father in heaven may also forgive you your trespasses.

MARK 11:25

Bearing with one another, and forgiving one another, if anyone has a complaint against another; even as Christ forgave you, so you also must do.

COLOSSIANS 3:13

Not returning evil for evil or reviling for reviling, but on the contrary blessing, knowing that you were called to this, that you may inherit a blessing.

1 PETER 3:9

Forgive us our sins, for we also forgive everyone who is indebted to us.

LUKE 11:4

Now may the God of patience and comfort grant you to be like-minded toward one another, according to Christ Jesus, that you may with one mind and one mouth glorify the God and Father of our Lord Jesus Christ. Therefore receive one another, just as Christ also received us, to the glory of God.

ROMANS 15:5-7

Do not remember the former things, nor consider the things of old.

ISAIAH 43:18

When He was reviled, did not revile in return; when He suffered, He did not threaten, but committed Himself to Him who judges righteously.

1 PETER 2:23

Let all bitterness, wrath, anger, clamor, and evil speaking be put away from you, with all malice. And be kind to one another, tenderhearted, forgiving one another, even as God in Christ forgave you.

EPHESIANS 4:31-32

PRAYER

HEAVENLY FATHER, *I choose to forgive anyone who has offended or hurt me. I release them into Your hands as their Judge, and I cancel any further debt or obligation they have toward me.*

Cleanse my heart today, Father. I let go of any anger or bitterness. I let go of my desire to be in control, and I submit to Your Lordship over every relationship and situation.

May my life reflect Your mercy and grace, Lord. May people come to know Your love as they see me forgive others through Your Spirit's work in my life.

In Jesus' name. **AMEN.**

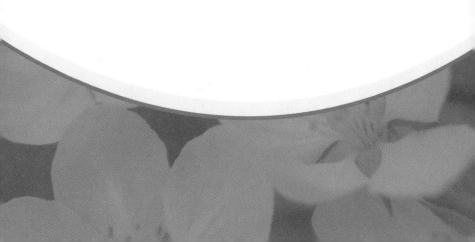

Present your bodies a living sacrifice,
holy, acceptable to God.
ROMANS 12:1

$\mathcal{S}$EXUAL SIN

WHAT THE BIBLE describes as sexual sin has now been accepted as "normal" by much of our culture. TV sitcoms are filled with premarital sex, adultery, and homosexuality, yet these programs never mention that such conduct is forbidden in God's Word.

Hebrews 13:4 warns: *"Marriage is honorable among all, and the bed undefiled; but fornicators and adulterers God will judge."*

Why does God tell us to abstain from sexual sin? Is it because He wants to keep us from enjoying life? No, quite the contrary—He's trying to *spare us* the inevitable pain and negative consequences that result from making the wrong choices.

Actually, our main focus should not be on the sin we're trying to avoid, but on developing an intimate relationship with the Lord so we can fulfill His calling: *"**Flee** also youthful lusts; but **pursue** righteousness, faith, love, peace with those who call on the Lord out of a pure heart"* (2 Timothy 2:22).

Flee sexual immorality. Every sin that a man does is outside the body, but he who commits sexual immorality sins against his own body. Or do you not know that your body is the temple of the Holy Spirit who is in you, whom you have from God, and you are not your own? For you were bought at a price; therefore glorify God in your body and in your spirit, which are God's.

1 CORINTHIANS 6:18-20

The works of the flesh are evident, which are: adultery, fornication, uncleanness, lewdness.

GALATIANS 5:19

He who covers his sins will not prosper, but whoever confesses and forsakes them will have mercy.

PROVERBS 28:13

Do you not know that the unrighteous will not inherit the kingdom of God? Do not be deceived. Neither fornicators, nor idolaters, nor adulterers, nor homosexuals, nor sodomites, nor thieves, nor covetous, nor drunkards, nor revilers, nor extortioners will inherit the kingdom of God.

1 CORINTHIANS 6:9-10

Whoever commits adultery with a woman lacks understanding; He who does so destroys his own soul. Wounds and dishonor he will get, and his reproach will not be wiped away.

PROVERBS 6:32-33

You shall not lie with a male as with a woman. It is an abomination.

LEVITICUS 18:22

SEXUAL SIN

You have heard that it was said to those of old, "You shall not commit adultery." But I say to you that whoever looks at a woman to lust for her has already committed adultery with her in his heart.

MATTHEW 5:27-28

This is the will of God, your sanctification: that you should abstain from sexual immorality; that each of you should know how to possess his own vessel in sanctification and honor, not in passion of lust, like the Gentiles who do not know God; that no one should take advantage of and defraud his brother in this matter, because the Lord is the avenger of all such, as we also forewarned you and testified. For God did not call us to uncleanness, but in holiness.

1 THESSALONIANS 4:3-7

God also gave them up to uncleanness, in the lusts of their hearts, to dishonor their bodies among themselves…God gave them up to vile passions. For even their women exchanged the natural use for what is against nature. Likewise also the men, leaving the natural use of the woman, burned in their lust for one another, men with men committing what is shameful, and receiving in themselves the penalty of their error which was due.

ROMANS 1:24-27

As He who called you is holy, you also be holy in all your conduct, because it is written, "Be holy, for I am holy."

1 PETER 1:15-16

PRAYER

DEAR FATHER, *I submit my body and my sexuality totally to You. Forgive me for any ways I've disobeyed Your precepts in the past. As David cried out to You after he sinned with Bathsheba, so I ask You today: "Create in me a clean heart, O God, and renew a steadfast spirit within me" (Psalm 51:10).*

Forgive me, Lord, for allowing my thinking and behavior to be influenced by the immoral mindset of this world. Transform me by the renewing of my mind as I study, meditate on, and obey Your Word.

Thank You for giving me a new beginning as I humble myself and submit to Your Lordship. I'm grateful for the hope and future You've set before me!

In Jesus' name. **AMEN.**

Your Maker is your husband, the Lord of hosts is His name;
and your Redeemer is the Holy One of Israel; He is called
the God of the whole earth. For the Lord has called you.

Isaiah 54:5-6

SINGLENESS

INSTEAD OF SEEING your singleness as something negative, embrace it today as a crucial training ground for God's calling on your life. For most people, God's future calling includes marriage (Genesis 2:18), but at times He calls people to a lifetime of singleness and celibacy (1 Corinthians 7:8).

One thing is for sure: God has great plans for your life (Jeremiah 29:11)! Because of that, you can *trust Him* with your future…your career…and your relationships.

On the one hand, we should be patient in our relationships, led by God's peace: *"Whoever believes will not act hastily"* (Isaiah 28:16). But there's also a time to cast off fear and boldly follow God's calling: *"Be strong and of good courage; do not be afraid, nor be dismayed, for the LORD your God is with you"* (Joshua 1:9).

Trust Him! Seek Him! Obey Him! He has good plans for you.

I will betroth you to Me forever; yes, I will betroth you to Me in righteousness and justice, in lovingkindness and mercy.

HOSEA 2:19

Do not fear, for you will not be ashamed; neither be disgraced, for you will not be put to shame; for you will forget the shame of your youth, and will not remember the reproach of your widowhood anymore. For your Maker is your husband, the LORD of hosts is His name; and your Redeemer is the Holy One of Israel; He is called the God of the whole earth. For the LORD has called you.

ISAIAH 54:4-6

Delight yourself also in the LORD, and He shall give you the desires of your heart.

PSALM 37:4

This is the will of God, your sanctification: that you should abstain from sexual immorality; that each of you should know how to possess his own vessel in sanctification and honor, not in passion of lust, like the Gentiles who do not know God; that no one should take advantage of and defraud his brother in this matter, because the Lord is the avenger of all such, as we also forewarned you and testified. For God did not call us to uncleanness, but in holiness.

1 THESSALONIANS 4:3-7

I say to the unmarried and to the widows: it is good for them if they remain even as I am.

1 CORINTHIANS 7:8

As God has distributed to each one, as the Lord has called each one, so let him walk.

1 CORINTHIANS 7:17

Are you bound to a wife? Do not seek to be loosed. Are you loosed from a wife? Do not seek a wife. But even if you do marry, you have not sinned; and if a virgin marries, she has not sinned. Nevertheless such will have trouble in the flesh, but I would spare you.

1 CORINTHIANS 7:27-28

Behold what manner of love the Father has bestowed on us…We know that when He is revealed, we shall be like Him, for we shall see Him as He is. And everyone who has this hope in Him purifies himself, just as He is pure.

1 JOHN 3:1-3

I want you to be without care. He who is unmarried cares for the things of the Lord—how he may please the Lord. But he who is married cares about the things of the world—how he may please his wife…And this I say for your own profit, not that I may put a leash on you, but for what is proper, and that you may serve the Lord without distraction.

1 CORINTHIANS 7:32-33,35

Marriage is honorable among all, and the bed undefiled; but fornicators and adulterers God will judge.

HEBREWS 13:4

PRAYER

HEAVENLY FATHER, *I trust my future to You.*
Lead me by Your peace. Keep me from being anxious or in a
hurry, and keep me from shrinking back in fear.

May You be the Lord of every relationship. May You be glorified
in how I spend my time. May my focus be on serving You and
pursuing Your Kingdom rather than on meeting my own needs.

Teach me, Lord, to delight myself in You, knowing I can trust
You to give me the desires of my heart. Thank You in
advance for meeting all my needs!

In Jesus' name. **AMEN.**

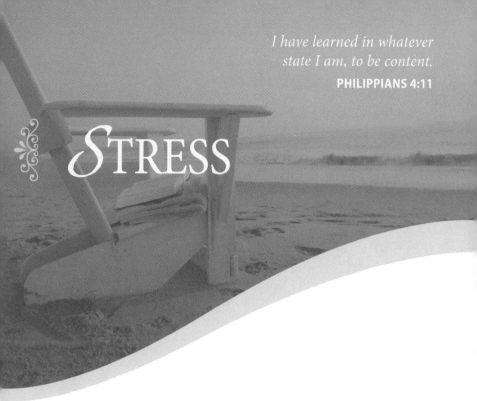

STRESS

WHILE SOME STRESS can be a positive force in our lives—causing us to turn to God and depend on His wisdom—most of us are carrying a huge bundle of stress the Lord never intended for us to shoulder.

Because God cares for us, He encourages us to cast all our cares upon Him (1 Peter 5:7). He doesn't say just SOME of our cares, He says ALL of them! This should eventually become a way of life for us, but often we need to make a *conscious decision* to surrender all of our concerns and burdens to the Lord.

Sometimes we assume all our heavy burdens are God's will for us, but often we're also carrying around concerns that are completely unnecessary. Remember: *"His commandments are not burdensome"* (1 John 5:3). He wants to shoulder your heavy load and give you rest!

Come to Me, all you who labor and are heavy laden, and I will give you rest. Take My yoke upon you and learn from Me, for I am gentle and lowly in heart, and you will find rest for your souls. For My yoke is easy and My burden is light.

MATTHEW 11:28-30

The beloved of the LORD shall dwell in safety by Him, Who shelters him all the day long; and he shall dwell between His shoulders.

DEUTERONOMY 33:12

The government will be upon His shoulder. And His name will be called Wonderful, Counselor, Mighty God, Everlasting Father, Prince of Peace.

ISAIAH 9:6

Jesus Himself stood in the midst of them, and said to them, "Peace to you."

LUKE 24:36

Be still, and know that I am God.

PSALM 46:10

The weapons of our warfare are not carnal but mighty in God for pulling down strongholds, casting down arguments and every high thing that exalts itself against the knowledge of God, bringing every thought into captivity to the obedience of Christ.

2 CORINTHIANS 10:4-5

Cast your burden on the LORD, and He shall sustain you.

PSALM 55:22

Peace I leave with you, My peace I give to you; not as the world gives do I give to you. Let not your heart be troubled, neither let it be afraid.

JOHN 14:27

Rejoice in the Lord always. Again I will say, rejoice! Let your gentleness be known to all men. The Lord is at hand.

Be anxious for nothing, but in everything by prayer and supplication, with thanksgiving, let your requests be made known to God; and the peace of God, which surpasses all understanding, will guard your hearts and minds through Christ Jesus.

Finally, brethren, whatever things are true, whatever things are noble, whatever things are just, whatever things are pure, whatever things are lovely, whatever things are of good report, if there is any virtue and if there is anything praiseworthy—meditate on these things.

The things which you learned and received and heard and saw in me, these do, and the God of peace will be with you.

PHILIPPIANS 4:4-9

PRAYER

FATHER, *I cast my cares and burdens on You today. Help me discern between the responsibilities You've truly ordained for me, and the ones I'm carrying unnecessarily.*

Lord, thank You for promising to give me the grace I need to handle every challenging situation You allow to come my way. I make a conscious decision to draw on Your grace and wisdom today.

Thank You for Your assurance that the battles of life are not mine to fight, but Yours. I thank You for lifting my spirits and promising me victory!

In Jesus' name. **AMEN.**

 TEMPTATION

GOD IS A GOD of new beginnings. He offers hope and transformation to all those who are serious about committing their lives to Him.

Many new Christians are confused when they face temptation from the enemy, thinking that the temptation *itself* is sin. However, even Jesus was tempted by Satan (Luke 4:1-13), and that is one of the very reasons He can help us overcome temptations in our own lives (Hebrews 2:18).

Although tempted, Jesus remained totally *"without sin"* (Hebrews 4:15). He wants to strengthen us today so that we, too, can stand against Satan's schemes. And God wants you to know that, even if you fall short at times, you can always come to Him for forgiveness and restoration (1 John 1:7-2:1).

Let him who thinks he stands take heed lest he fall. No temptation has overtaken you except such as is common to man; but God is faithful, who will not allow you to be tempted beyond what you are able, but with the temptation will also make the way of escape, that you may be able to bear it.

1 CORINTHIANS 10:12-13

Submit to God. Resist the devil and he will flee from you.

JAMES 4:7

For in that He Himself has suffered, being tempted, He is able to aid those who are tempted.

HEBREWS 2:18

We do not have a High Priest who cannot sympathize with our weaknesses, but was in all points tempted as we are, yet without sin. Let us therefore come boldly to the throne of grace, that we may obtain mercy and find grace to help in time of need.

HEBREWS 4:15-16

Your word I have hidden in my heart, that I might not sin against You.

PSALM 119:11

Let no one say when he is tempted, "I am tempted by God"; for God cannot be tempted by evil, nor does He Himself tempt anyone. But each one is tempted when he is drawn away by his own desires and enticed.

JAMES 1:13-14

He who covers his sins will not prosper, but whoever confesses and forsakes them will have mercy.

PROVERBS 28:13

I will behave wisely in a perfect way…I will set nothing wicked before my eyes…A perverse heart shall depart from me…My eyes shall be on the faithful of the land, that they may dwell with me…He who works deceit shall not dwell within my house; He who tells lies shall not continue in my presence.

PSALM 101:2-7

You are of God, little children, and have overcome them, because He who is in you is greater than he who is in the world.

1 JOHN 4:4

Now to Him who is able to keep you from stumbling, and to present you faultless before the presence of His glory with exceeding joy, to God our Savior, who alone is wise, be glory and majesty, dominion and power, both now and forever. Amen.

JUDE 24-25

My brethren, be strong in the Lord and in the power of His might. Put on the whole armor of God, that you may be able to stand against the wiles of the devil…Above all, taking the shield of faith with which you will be able to quench all the fiery darts of the wicked one.

EPHESIANS 6:10-11, 16

PRAYER

HEAVENLY FATHER, *give me discernment when faced by the schemes of the enemy. I thank You that Jesus' blood has the power to cleanse me from unrighteousness and protect me from temptation.*

Father, thank You for promising me everything I need for victory. I'm grateful that You're empowering me by Your Holy Spirit and giving me courage to escape the chains of sin. Give me the strength and grace I need each day to overcome temptation and the snares of the evil one.

Today I declare that Your Word is true, and I claim Your promises of cleansing, protection, and freedom. Thank You for Your faithfulness in bringing me to freedom!

In Jesus' name. **AMEN.**

WIDOWHOOD

GOD SEEMS TO have a special place in His heart for widows, for they have a prominent role throughout the Scriptures. Here are just a few examples of widows who played an important role in God's purposes: Ruth and Naomi (Ruth 1:1-5), the widow of Zarephath (1 Kings 17:8-16), Anna the prophetess (Luke 2:36-38), and the poor widow who gave her last two coins into the Temple treasury (Luke 21:1-4).

Although God is exalted *"in His holy habitation,"* He takes time to be *"a father of the fatherless"* and *"a defender of widows"* (Psalm 68:5). This ministry is so important that God calls it *"pure and undefiled religion"* (James 1:27)!

Widows are important to God! If you have lost your spouse, be encouraged that God wants to use you in a special way to fulfill His End-Time purposes!

Pure and undefiled religion before God and the Father is this: to visit orphans and widows in their trouble, and to keep oneself unspotted from the world.

JAMES 1:27

He administers justice for the fatherless and the widow, and loves the stranger, giving him food and clothing.

DEUTERONOMY 10:18

The LORD will destroy the house of the proud, but He will establish the boundary of the widow.

PROVERBS 15:25

Learn to do good; seek justice, rebuke the oppressor; defend the fatherless, plead for the widow.

ISAIAH 1:17

The LORD watches over the strangers; He relieves the fatherless and widow; but the way of the wicked He turns upside down.

PSALM 146:9

Do not fear, for you will not be ashamed; neither be disgraced, for you will not be put to shame; for you will forget the shame of your youth, and will not remember the reproach of your widowhood anymore. For your Maker is your husband, the LORD of hosts is His name; and your Redeemer is the Holy One of Israel; He is called the God of the whole earth…For the mountains shall depart and the hills be removed, but My kindness shall not depart from you, nor shall My covenant of peace be removed.

ISAIAH 54:4-5, 10

A wife is bound by law as long as her husband lives; but if her husband dies, she is at liberty to be married to whom she wishes, only in the Lord.

1 CORINTHIANS 7:39

I caused the widow's heart to sing for joy.

JOB 29:13

"Cursed is the one who perverts the justice due the stranger, the fatherless, and widow." And all the people shall say, "Amen!"

DEUTERONOMY 27:19

You now have sorrow; but I will see you again and your heart will rejoice, and your joy no one will take from you.

JOHN 16:22

You have turned for me my mourning into dancing; You have put off my sackcloth and clothed me with gladness.

PSALM 30:11

A father of the fatherless, a defender of widows, is God in His holy habitation.

PSALM 68:5

I will betroth you to Me forever; yes, I will betroth you to Me in righteousness and justice, in lovingkindness and mercy; I will betroth you to Me in faithfulness, and you shall know the LORD.

HOSEA 2:19-20

PRAYER

FATHER, *thank You for Your encouragement about the high calling widows have to serve Your Kingdom and fulfill Your purposes! I cast off discouragement today and rise up to fulfill my destiny in You.*

Thank You for the great examples in Your Word of widows who gave all they had because of their love for You. I trust You today to use and multiply my time, talent, and treasure for Your Kingdom.

Lord, I am trusting You to increase the length and impact of my life. Fill me afresh with Your Holy Spirit so I can take bold steps of faith!

In Jesus' name. **AMEN.**

GOD'S PROMISES
for
WHAT TO DO
WHEN YOU'RE…

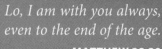

ᗌESERTED BY LOVED ONES

IF YOU'VE BEEN rejected or deserted by a friend or loved one, Jesus knows exactly how you feel. He had the same experience when His disciple Judas Iscariot betrayed Him and His other disciples forsook Him and fled.

Was this betrayal of Jesus a random event, outside the Father's loving control? Not at all. In fact, this experience was foretold in a Messianic psalm hundreds of years earlier: *"Even my own familiar friend in whom I trusted, who ate my bread, has lifted up his heel against me"* (Psalm 41:9).

This psalm continues with a wonderful word of encouragement for all who have suffered abandonment or betrayal: *"You, O Lord, be merciful to me, and raise me up"* (v. 10). No matter what kind of unfair treatment you've received from a loved one, God's plan is to be merciful to you and RAISE YOU UP!

When my father and my mother forsake me, then the LORD will take care of me.
PSALM 27:10

I have been young, and now am old; yet I have not seen the righteous forsaken, nor his descendants begging bread. He is ever merciful, and lends; and his descendants are blessed.
PSALM 37:25-26

Whereas you have been forsaken and hated...
I will make you an eternal excellence, a joy of many generations.
ISAIAH 60:15

The LORD will not cast off His people, nor will He forsake His inheritance.
PSALM 94:14

You shall no longer be termed Forsaken, nor shall your land any more be termed Desolate; but you shall be called Hephzibah, and your land Beulah; for the LORD delights in you, and your land shall be married.
ISAIAH 62:4

The LORD your God is a merciful God. He will not forsake you nor destroy you, nor forget the covenant of your fathers which He swore to them.
DEUTERONOMY 4:31

You are God, ready to pardon, gracious and merciful, slow to anger, abundant in kindness, and did not forsake them.
NEHEMIAH 9:17

Can a woman forget her nursing child, and not have compassion on the son of her womb? Surely they may forget, yet I will not forget you. See, I have inscribed you on the palms of My hands; Your walls are continually before Me.

ISAIAH 49:15-16

Be strong and of good courage, do not fear nor be afraid of them; for the LORD your God, He is the One who goes with you. He will not leave you nor forsake you.

DEUTERONOMY 31:6

The LORD will not forsake His people, for His great name's sake, because it has pleased the LORD to make you His people.

1 SAMUEL 12:22

It is better to trust in the LORD than to put confidence in man.

PSALM 118:8

Surely your salvation is coming; behold, His reward is with Him, and His work before Him. And they shall call them The Holy People, The Redeemed of the LORD; and you shall be called Sought Out, A City Not Forsaken.

ISAIAH 62:11-12

Those who know Your name will trust in You; for You, LORD, have not forsaken those who seek You.

PSALM 9:10

PRAYER

FATHER, *Your Word says You are able to work all things together for good to those who love You. I call on You today to honor Your promise and work these painful circumstances for my good and for Your glory.*

Thank You, Lord, that nothing is outside of Your knowledge or control. In the midst of every difficult experience, You are able to fulfill Your purposes and lift me up!

Father, I forgive all those who have treated me unfairly, just as You have graciously forgiven me for the ways my actions have sometimes hurt You. Thank You for opening my eyes to new hope for restoration and victory!

In Jesus' name. **AMEN.**

Love one another fervently
with a pure heart.
1 PETER 1:22

Experiencing Marital Problems

JESUS SAID He would build His church on such a strong foundation that *"the gates of hell"* would not be able to prevail against it (Matthew 16:18), and He wants to build our marriages on that same kind of foundation—the foundation of His Word.

If your marriage is struggling today, it probably would be easy to find someone or something to blame. Perhaps there are financial problems...or infidelity...or substance abuse... or uncontrolled anger...or some other factor that has brought your relationship to a crisis point.

But Proverbs 24:3 makes an important statement about what it takes to have a strong marriage and family: *"Through wisdom a house is built, and by understanding it is established."* In order to have a healthy marriage, we need God's wisdom and understanding!

Wives, submit to your own husbands, as to the Lord. For the husband is head of the wife, as also Christ is head of the church; and He is the Savior of the body.

Therefore, just as the church is subject to Christ, so let the wives be to their own husbands in everything. Husbands, love your wives, just as Christ also loved the church and gave Himself for her, that He might sanctify and cleanse her with the washing of water by the word, that He might present her to Himself a glorious church, not having spot or wrinkle or any such thing, but that she should be holy and without blemish. So husbands ought to love their own wives as their own bodies; he who loves his wife loves himself…

Let each one of you in particular so love his own wife as himself, and let the wife see that she respects her husband.

EPHESIANS 5:22-28, 33

The LORD God said, "It is not good that man should be alone; I will make him a helper comparable to him."

GENESIS 2:18

A man shall leave his father and mother and be joined to his wife, and they shall become one flesh.

GENESIS 2:24

Let each man have his own wife, and let each woman have her own husband. Let the husband render to his wife the affection due her, and likewise also the wife to her husband.

1 CORINTHIANS 7:2-3

Wives, likewise, be submissive to your own husbands, that even if some do not obey the word, they, without a word, may be won by the conduct of their wives…Husbands, likewise, dwell with them with understanding, giving honor to the wife, as to the weaker vessel, and as being heirs together of the grace of life, that your prayers may not be hindered.

1 Peter 3:1, 7

All of you be of one mind, having compassion for one another; love as brothers, be tenderhearted, be courteous; not returning evil for evil or reviling for reviling, but on the contrary blessing, knowing that you were called to this, that you may inherit a blessing.

1 Peter 3:8-9

Let all bitterness, wrath, anger, clamor, and evil speaking be put away from you, with all malice. And be kind to one another, tenderhearted, forgiving one another, even as God in Christ forgave you.

Ephesians 4:31-32

Love suffers long and is kind; love does not envy; love does not parade itself, is not puffed up; does not behave rudely, does not seek its own, is not provoked, thinks no evil; does not rejoice in iniquity, but rejoices in the truth; bears all things, believes all things, hopes all things, endures all things. Love never fails.

1 Corinthians 13:4-8

PRAYER

FATHER, *I acknowledge today that You are the One who created marriage, and You're the One who knows how to fix marriages when they're struggling. Forgive me for the ways I've failed to seek Your wisdom and obey Your instructions for my marriage. I acknowledge that my own ways have failed, and I need Your help and wisdom to bring healing to my marriage.*

Today I recommit myself to Your Lordship. I ask You to change my heart and rekindle the love in my marriage. I look to You as the only reliable source for unselfish love.

Show me Your ways, Lord, so my home is built on a firm foundation. Thank You for giving me hope today—the hope that can only come from You.

In Jesus' name. **AMEN.**

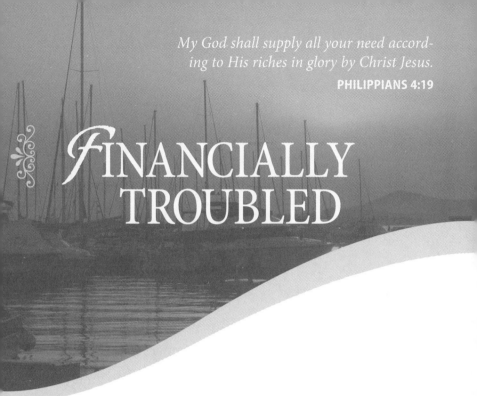

$\mathscr{F}$INANCIALLY TROUBLED

GOD HAS A PLAN for your finances. His heart is to bless His children, so they can be a blessing to others (Genesis 12:2)!

Your primary need today is to truly **seek HIM**, for His Word promises, *"Those who seek the LORD shall not lack any good thing"* (Psalm 34:10). Whatever you need from your Heavenly Father, He wants to give you—but you must ask...seek...and knock until your breakthrough comes (Matthew 7:7).

Don't sit back passively, hoping God's provision will come. You must be aggressive and fight for it, crying out to Him until you receive the provision you need.

Remember: If you're expecting a miracle financial harvest from God, you must first trust Him by sowing financial seeds into His Kingdom (Luke 6:38). If you're in *need*, sow a *seed*—for hoarding leads to poverty and lack.

Beloved, I pray that you may prosper in all things and be in health, just as your soul prospers.

3 JOHN 1:2

I have been young, and now am old; yet I have not seen the righteous forsaken, nor his descendants begging bread.

PSALM 37:25

"Bring all the tithes into the storehouse, that there may be food in My house, and try Me now in this," says the LORD of hosts, "If I will not open for you the windows of heaven and pour out for you such blessing that there will not be room enough to receive it. And I will rebuke the devourer for your sakes."

MALACHI 3:10-11

All these blessings shall come upon you and overtake you, because you obey the voice of the LORD your God...The LORD will grant you plenty of goods, in the fruit of your body, in the increase of your livestock, and in the produce of your ground, in the land of which the LORD swore to your fathers to give you.

The LORD will open to you His good treasure, the heavens, to give the rain to your land in its season, and to bless all the work of your hand. You shall lend to many nations, but you shall not borrow. And the LORD will make you the head and not the tail; you shall be above only, and not be beneath, if you heed the commandments of the LORD your God, which I command you today, and are careful to observe them.

DEUTERONOMY 28:2, 11-13

He who sows sparingly will also reap sparingly, and he who sows bountifully will also reap bountifully...And God is able to make all grace abound toward you, that you, always having all sufficiency in all things, may have an abundance for every good work.

2 CORINTHIANS 9:6-8

God gives wisdom and knowledge and joy to a man who is good in His sight; but to the sinner He gives the work of gathering and collecting, that he may give to him who is good before God.

ECCLESIASTES 2:26

The LORD is my shepherd; I shall not want.

PSALM 23:1

The LORD your God is bringing you into a good land, a land of brooks of water, of fountains and springs, that flow out of valleys and hills; a land of wheat and barley, of vines and fig trees and pomegranates, a land of olive oil and honey; a land in which you will eat bread without scarcity, in which you will lack nothing...

When you have eaten and are full, then you shall bless the LORD your God for the good land which He has given you...remember the LORD your God, for it is He who gives you power to get wealth, that He may establish His covenant which He swore to your fathers, as it is this day.

DEUTERONOMY 8:7-10, 18

PRAYER

HEAVENLY *Father, You know the financial needs and other concerns I'm facing today. Yet my greatest need is simply to seek You and know You more intimately.*

Acknowledging You as my Shepherd and Provider, I bring You my tithes and offerings. Your Word says You're bringing me into a "good land" where I will lack nothing, for You give me the power to produce wealth.

When my financial breakthrough comes, I pledge to honor you with the "first fruits" and give You glory for Your blessings. As You bless me, Lord, I also pray You will make me a greater blessing to others.

In Jesus' name. **AMEN.**

GRIEVING

IF YOU'RE GRIEVING over the death of a loved one today, God wants you to enter His presence and find a place of peace and safety. Let Him comfort you with His loving embrace and restore His joy to your soul.

God will not leave you alone in your sadness. He promises to be right there with you even as you *"walk through the valley of the shadow of death"* (Psalm 23:4).

The Bible says God offers special healing balm for those who grieve, giving them *"beauty for ashes, the oil of joy for mourning"* (Isaiah 61:3). Yes, there may be weeping and pain for a season, but He promises that a better day is ahead, a day of renewed hope and joy: *"He will swallow up death forever, and the LORD God will wipe away tears from all faces"* (Isaiah 25:8).

I do not want you to be ignorant, brethren, concerning those who have fallen asleep, lest you sorrow as others who have no hope. For if we believe that Jesus died and rose again, even so God will bring with Him those who sleep in Jesus… For the Lord Himself will descend from heaven with a shout, with the voice of an archangel, and with the trumpet of God. And the dead in Christ will rise first. Then we who are alive and remain shall be caught up together with them in the clouds to meet the Lord in the air. And thus we shall always be with the Lord. Therefore comfort one another with these words.

1 Thessalonians 4:13-18

The LORD is near to those who have a broken heart.

Psalm 34:18

We are confident, yes, well pleased rather to be absent from the body and to be present with the Lord.

2 Corinthians 5:8

Yea, though I walk through the valley of the shadow of death, I will fear no evil; for You are with me; Your rod and Your staff, they comfort me.

Psalm 23:4

When you pass through the waters, I will be with you; and through the rivers, they shall not overflow you. When you walk through the fire, you shall not be burned, nor shall the flame scorch you.

Isaiah 43:2

Blessed be the God and Father of our Lord Jesus Christ, the Father of mercies and God of all comfort, who comforts us in all our tribulation, that we may be able to comfort those who are in any trouble, with the comfort with which we ourselves are comforted by God.

2 CORINTHIANS 1:3-4

He has sent Me to heal the brokenhearted...to console those who mourn in Zion, to give them beauty for ashes, the oil of joy for mourning, the garment of praise for the spirit of heaviness; that they may be called trees of righteousness, the planting of the LORD, that He may be glorified.

ISAIAH 61:1-3

O Death, where is your sting? O Hades, where is your victory? The sting of death is sin, and the strength of sin is the law. But thanks be to God, who gives us the victory through our Lord Jesus Christ.

1 CORINTHIANS 15:55-57

The LORD has comforted His people, and will have mercy on His afflicted.

ISAIAH 49:13

God will wipe away every tear from their eyes; there shall be no more death, nor sorrow, nor crying. There shall be no more pain, for the former things have passed away.

REVELATION 21:4

PRAYER

LORD, *You have walked through the valley of death, and You know the way. In this time of sorrow, lead me to Your secret place of comfort and healing. Sustain me with Your love, and restore peace to my soul.*

You are near to those who are brokenhearted, and I need You to wrap Your strong and comforting arms around me today. Replace my ashes with Your beauty, my pain with Your purpose, and my heavy heart with Your oil of joy.

Lord, bring me through this dark valley to a new day of hope and peace. As You are comforting and blessing me, use me to be a blessing to others.

In Jesus' name. **AMEN.**

OVERWHELMED BY CIRCUMSTANCES

WE ARE NOT promised a trouble-free life in this world, but we ARE promised God will be with us all along the way. He promises to lead us to victory if we put our trust in Him (2 Corinthians 2:14).

Trust God today. Fix your eyes on Him instead of on your circumstances. As you do, you'll find Him to be trustworthy—even in your darkest hours.

Remember: The Lord is right there with you! Draw near to Him, and He has promised to draw near to you (James 4:7-8). The throne room of God is open to you, and He beckons you to come.

The LORD is good,
a stronghold in the day
of trouble; and He knows
those who trust in Him.

NAHUM 1:7

When my heart is over-
whelmed; lead me to the
rock that is higher than I.

PSALM 61:2

The waters would have
overwhelmed us, the stream
would have gone over our
soul; then the swollen waters
would have gone over our
soul…Our help is in the
name of the LORD, who
made heaven and earth.

PSALM 124:4-5, 8

Let not your heart be
troubled; you believe in
God, believe also in Me.

JOHN 14:1

We are hard-pressed on
every side, yet not crushed;
we are perplexed, but not in
despair; persecuted, but not
forsaken; struck down, but
not destroyed.

2 CORINTHIANS 4:8-9

Though I walk in the midst
of trouble, You will revive
me; You will stretch out
Your hand against the wrath
of my enemies, and Your
right hand will save me.

PSALM 138:7

When you pass through the
waters, I will be with you;
and through the rivers,
they shall not overflow you.
When you walk through
the fire, you shall not be
burned, nor shall the flame
scorch you.

ISAIAH 43:2

OVERWHELMED BY CIRCUMSTANCES

We know that all things work together for good to those who love God, to those who are the called according to His purpose.

ROMANS 8:28

I will be glad and rejoice in Your mercy, for You have considered my trouble; You have known my soul in adversities.

PSALM 31:7

I will lift up my eyes to the hills—from whence comes my help? My help comes from the LORD, who made heaven and earth.

PSALM 121:1-2

Therefore do not worry about tomorrow, for tomorrow will worry about its own things. Sufficient for the day is its own trouble.

MATTHEW 6:34

If it had not been the LORD who was on our side, when men rose up against us, then they would have swallowed us alive, when their wrath was kindled against us; then the waters would have overwhelmed us, the stream would have gone over our soul; then the swollen waters would have gone over our soul.

Blessed be the LORD, who has not given us as prey to their teeth. Our soul has escaped as a bird from the snare of the fowlers; the snare is broken, and we have escaped.

PSALM 124:6-7

PRAYER

FATHER, *I need to hear Your strong and comforting voice today. My problems seem overwhelming, but I choose to fix my gaze on You. I choose to trust in Your mighty power and Your faithfulness.*

Come to my aid, Lord. Lead me to the rock that is higher than I. Teach me to find shelter in the secret place of Your presence.

I know that nothing will happen today that is outside Your knowledge and control. This is the day You have made, and I will rejoice and be glad in it!

In Jesus' name. **AMEN.**

> *Heal me, O LORD, and I shall be healed;*
> *save me, and I shall be saved,*
> *for You are my praise.*
>
> **JEREMIAH 17:14**

SICK

WHILE MOST PEOPLE today accept disease and death as "normal" parts of life, they were never God's original intention. When the world was first created, the Bible records, *"Then God saw everything that He had made, and indeed it was very good"* (Genesis 1:31). Disease and death only entered the world after Adam and Eve disobeyed the Lord and allowed satanic forces to gain a foothold on humankind (Genesis 3).

When Jesus came to earth, He announced that God's Kingdom was at hand. He healed the sick, cast out demons, fed the multitudes, and raised the dead. All of this was a demonstration of the blessings God intended at His original creation.

If you or a loved one is in need of healing today, remember that Jesus is your Great Physician. When He preached the Gospel of the Kingdom, He healed *"ALL kinds of sickness and ALL kinds of disease"* (Matthew 4:23). So no matter what *kind* of healing you might need, Jesus is ready to be your Healer!

Beloved, I pray that you may prosper in all things and be in health, just as your soul prospers.

3 JOHN 1:2

Jesus went about all the cities and villages, teaching in their synagogues, preaching the gospel of the kingdom, and healing every sickness and every disease among the people.

MATTHEW 9:35

The whole multitude sought to touch Him, for power went out from Him and healed them all.

LUKE 6:19

Jesus Christ is the same yesterday, today, and forever.

HEBREWS 13:8

Bless the Lord, O my soul, and forget not all His benefits: who forgives all your iniquities, who heals all your diseases.

PSALM 103:2-3

If you diligently heed the voice of the Lord your God and do what is right in His sight, give ear to His commandments and keep all His statutes, I will put none of the diseases on you which I have brought on the Egyptians. For I am the Lord who heals you.

EXODUS 15:26

He was wounded for our transgressions, He was bruised for our iniquities; the chastisement for our peace was upon Him, and by His stripes we are healed.

ISAIAH 53:5

My son, give attention to my words; incline your ear to my sayings. Do not let them depart from your eyes; keep them in the midst of your heart; for they are life to those who find them, and health to all their flesh.

PROVERBS 4:20-22

He sent His word and healed them, and delivered them from their destructions.

PSALM 107:20

Is anyone among you sick? Let him call for the elders of the church, and let them pray over him, anointing him with oil in the name of the Lord. And the prayer of faith will save the sick, and the Lord will raise him up. And if he has committed sins, he will be forgiven.

JAMES 5:14-15

These signs will follow those who believe…They will lay hands on the sick, and they will recover.

MARK 16:17-18

He was wounded for our transgressions, He was bruised for our iniquities; the chastisement for our peace was upon Him, and by His stripes we are healed.

ISAIAH 53:5

If the Spirit of Him who raised Jesus from the dead dwells in you, He who raised Christ from the dead will also give life to your mortal bodies through His Spirit who dwells in you.

ROMANS 8:11

PRAYER

LORD JESUS, *You are the same yesterday, today, and forever, and nothing is too difficult for You! I bring You my physical ailment today, asking for You to mightily intervene with Your healing power. Manifest Your Kingdom and replace disease with wholeness.*

Send Your Word and heal me, Lord. Deliver me from every attack of the enemy. I declare that You died for my sicknesses as well as for my sins!

I give You praise in advance for touching my body and restoring me to health. May You be glorified through my body as Your holy temple!

In Your name. **AMEN.**

*S*PIRITUALLY LUKEWARM

PERHAPS YOU'RE AT a place in your life today when you're crying out to God, as David once did: *"Restore to me the joy of Your salvation!"* (Psalm 51:12). The Lord heard David's prayer, and He hears *yours* as well.

Sometimes we can allow the cares and busyness of life to rob us of our peace and joy. Instead of the abundant life God intends for us, we experience drudgery and discouragement. Life becomes a rat race, and we lose sight of our calling and purpose in the Lord.

Come before God with a humble heart today, and ask Him to restore your *"first love"* relationship with Him (Revelation 2:4). He will give you His joy, rekindle your passion, and set you free from lukewarm living!

Break up your fallow ground, for it is time to seek the Lord, till He comes and rains righteousness on you.

HOSEA 10:12

I know your works, that you are neither cold nor hot. I could wish you were cold or hot. So then, because you are lukewarm, and neither cold nor hot, I will vomit you out of My mouth. Because you say, "I am rich, have become wealthy, and have need of nothing"—and do not know that you are wretched, miserable, poor, blind, and naked—I counsel you to buy from Me gold refined in the fire, that you may be rich; and white garments, that you may be clothed, that the shame of your nakedness may not be revealed; and anoint your eyes with eye salve, that you may see. As many as I love, I rebuke and chasten. Therefore be zealous and repent.

Behold, I stand at the door and knock. If anyone hears My voice and opens the door, I will come in to him and dine with him, and he with Me. To him who overcomes I will grant to sit with Me on My throne, as I also overcame and sat down with My Father on His throne. He who has an ear, let him hear.

REVELATION 3:15-22

Stand in the ways and see, and ask for the old paths, where the good way is, and walk in it; then you will find rest for your souls.

JEREMIAH 6:16

My anger has turned away from him.

HOSEA 14:4

I will heal their backsliding, I will love them freely, for

"Return to Me, and I will return to you," says the Lord of hosts.

MALACHI 3:7

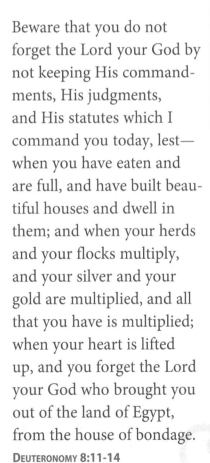

Beware that you do not forget the Lord your God by not keeping His command-ments, His judgments, and His statutes which I command you today, lest—when you have eaten and are full, and have built beau-tiful houses and dwell in them; and when your herds and your flocks multiply, and your silver and your gold are multiplied, and all that you have is multiplied; when your heart is lifted up, and you forget the Lord your God who brought you out of the land of Egypt, from the house of bondage.

DEUTERONOMY 8:11-14

The backslider in heart will be filled with his own ways, but a good man will be satisfied from above.

PROVERBS 14:14

Today, if you will hear His voice, do not harden your hearts…Beware, brethren, lest there be in any of you an evil heart of unbelief in departing from the living God; but exhort one anoth-er daily, while it is called "Today," lest any of you be hardened through the deceitfulness of sin.

For we have become partak-ers of Christ if we hold the beginning of our confidence steadfast to the end.

HEBREWS 3:7-8, 12-14

PRAYER

FATHER, *restore my passion for You and Your purposes. Deliver me from apathy and lukewarmness. Remove anything in my life that is hindering my intimacy with You.*

Lord, forgive me for the earthbound perspective I've had. Instead of living for the things of this world, I want my life to reflect Your eternal purposes.

I'm tired of just going through the motions in my Christian life. Take me off my treadmill of mediocre living and give me new vision for my destiny in You. I want to impact lives for Your Kingdom!

In Jesus' name. **AMEN.**

UNCERTAIN ABOUT GOD'S WAYS

THE BIBLE MAKES two important points about our knowledge of God's ways. On the one hand, His ways are clearly higher than our ways. But the Bible also reveals God's desire to show us His ways. Realizing this, David prayed, *"Show me Your ways, O LORD; teach me Your paths"* (Psalm 25:4). And amazingly, the apostle Paul states, *"We have the mind of Christ"* (1 Corinthians 2:16).

God wants to show you His ways. He wants to reveal His great plan and purpose for your life! But you have a role to play in this too.

Take time to study and meditate on God's Word. Set aside a special time and place each day when you can come into His presence and listen to His voice. Keep a journal of the direction He gives you for your life, and commit yourself to following His instructions. The more you trust and obey Him, the more He will unfold a revelation of His will for you!

"My thoughts are not your thoughts, nor are your ways My ways," says the Lord. "For as the heavens are higher than the earth, so are My ways higher than your ways, and My thoughts than your thoughts."

ISAIAH 55:8-9

Oh, the depth of the riches both of the wisdom and knowledge of God! How unsearchable are His judgments and His ways past finding out! "For who has known the mind of the Lord? Or who has become His counselor? Or who has first given to Him and it shall be repaid to him?" For of Him and through Him and to Him are all things, to whom be glory forever.

ROMANS 11:33-36

Eye has not seen, nor ear heard, nor have entered into the heart of man the things which God has prepared for those who love Him. But God has revealed them to us through His Spirit.

1 CORINTHIANS 2:9-10

The secret things belong to the Lord our God, but those things which are revealed belong to us and to our children forever, that we may do all the words of this law.

DEUTERONOMY 29:29

We know that all things work together for good to those who love God, to those who are the called according to His purpose.

ROMANS 8:28

Let us hold fast the confession of our hope without wavering, for He who promised is faithful.

HEBREWS 10:23

Show me Your ways, O LORD; teach me Your paths. Lead me in Your truth and teach me, for You are the God of my salvation; on You I wait all the day.

PSALM 25:4-5

Come, and let us go up to the mountain of the LORD, to the house of the God of Jacob; He will teach us His ways, and we shall walk in His paths.

ISAIAH 2:3

I will make an everlasting covenant with them, that I will not turn away from doing them good.

JEREMIAH 32:40

The Lord will perfect that which concerns me; Your mercy, O Lord, endures forever; do not forsake the works of Your hands.

PSALM 138:8

He has shown you, O man, what is good; and what does the LORD require of you but to do justly, to love mercy, and to walk humbly with your God?

MICAH 6:8

Fear not, for I am with you; be not dismayed, for I am your God. I will strengthen you, yes, I will help you, I will uphold you with My righteous right hand.

ISAIAH 41:10

PRAYER

LORD, *I want to know You better.*
I want to hear Your voice and walk in Your ways.

Thank You for giving me Your Word as a roadmap for my life.
Thank You that You want to reveal Your will and open my eyes to
the hope of my calling. Thank You for allowing me to hear the voice
of Your Spirit and gain a greater portion of the mind of Christ.

Lord, I want to walk in confidence and faith rather than
uncertainty and fear. Give me the courage I need to take
bold steps of faith toward Your destiny for my life!

In Jesus' name. **AMEN.**

WAITING ON GOD

ALMOST NOTHING is as difficult for most people as *waiting*. Whether we're waiting in rush hour traffic or in a grocery store line, impatience—or even anger—can engulf us.

However, God repeatedly tells us in His Word that we are to *wait* on Him. This means taking time to enter into His presence to worship Him…listen…meditate…and share our heart.

Why is this so important? Waiting is a key that unlocks greater intimacy with Him. And the Bible describes many amazing benefits for those who take time to wait on the Lord: strength, hope, courage, provision, guidance, encouragement, and vision. All these—and more—are the rewards you'll receive when you wait on God!

Have you not known? Have you not heard? The everlasting God, the LORD, the Creator of the ends of the earth, neither faints nor is weary. His understanding is unsearchable.

He gives power to the weak, and to those who have no might He increases strength. Even the youths shall faint and be weary, and the young men shall utterly fall.

Those who wait on the Lord shall renew their strength; they shall mount up with wings like eagles, they shall run and not be weary, they shall walk and not faint.

ISAIAH 40:28-31

Wait on the Lord; be of good courage, and He shall strengthen your heart. Wait, I say, on the Lord!

PSALM 27:14

Lead me in Your truth and teach me, for You are the God of my salvation; on You I wait all the day.

PSALM 25:5

Our soul waits for the Lord; He is our help and our shield.

PSALM 33:20

The eyes of all look expectantly to You, and You give them their food in due season. You open Your hand and satisfy the desire of every living thing.

PSALM 145:15-16

I wait for the Lord, my soul waits, and in His word I do hope.

PSALM 130:5

I would have lost heart, unless I had believed that I would see the goodness of the Lord in the land of the living. Wait on the Lord; be of good courage, and He shall strengthen your heart; wait, I say, on the Lord!

PSALM 27:13-14

This I recall to my mind, therefore I have hope. Through the LORD's mercies we are not consumed, because His compassions fail not. They are new every morning; great is Your faithfulness. "The LORD is my portion," says my soul, "Therefore I hope in Him!" The LORD is good to those who wait for Him, to the soul who seeks Him. It is good that one should hope and wait quietly for the salvation of the LORD.

LAMENTATIONS 3:21-26

I will stand my watch and set myself on the rampart, and watch to see what He will say to me, and what I will answer when I am corrected.

The Lord answered me and said: "Write the vision and make it plain on tablets, that he may run who reads it.

For the vision is yet for an appointed time; but at the end it will speak, and it will not lie. Though it tarries, wait for it; because it will surely come, it will not tarry.

HABAKKUK 2:1-3

Indeed, let no one who waits on You be ashamed…Show me Your ways, O Lord; teach me Your paths.

PSALM 25:3-4

PRAYER

FATHER, *still my anxious heart and teach me to wait on You.
I need You so much. Help me mount up like an eagle
that is soaring to new heights.*

*Lord, I need fresh vision for my life. Show me Your ways, and show
me Your plans for me. As I wait on You, give me new strength and
courage to carry out Your will.*

*Help me take time to meet with You every day, Lord.
I celebrate this day of new beginnings in my relationship with You.*

In Jesus' name. **AMEN.**

YOU CAN BE SAVED BY GOD'S AMAZING GRACE!

THE BIBLE SAYS, *"If you confess with your mouth the Lord Jesus and believe in your heart that God raised Him from the dead, you will be saved"* (Romans 10:9).

When you *do* confess and believe these truths, you'll receive God's gift of eternal life! You'll have a home in Heaven with Him after you die, *and* you'll also receive the covenant blessings of His Peace, presence, Power, Protection, and Provision here on earth.

If you've never asked Jesus to be the Lord of your life, just pray this simple prayer right now:

Dear Jesus,

I need You. I confess that I'm a sinner and that You are holy. Jesus, I believe you are God's Son and that He raised You from the dead.

Thank You for dying on the Cross for me and for providing

the only way for me to have a relationship with God. Please forgive me for all my sins, and wash me clean with Your blood. Come and live in my heart now, and fill me with Your Holy Spirit.

Thank You for rescuing me and giving me the opportunity to live in Heaven with You forever. Please be the Lord of my life. Teach me how to love You and walk with You every day.

I pray this in Your name. Amen.

If you just prayed this prayer, you have been "born again" and saved by God's amazing grace. The angels in Heaven are rejoicing right now over *you!* Welcome to the family of God.

As you begin your new life with Jesus, make sure to spend time with Him every day. Talk to Him. Sit quietly and listen for the voice of His Holy Spirit to speak to you.

As you grow and mature in your new faith and your knowledge of the Bible, you will learn to recognize the Lord's voice speaking to you in your mind and heart. He will bring you wonderful comfort and direction for your life as you gain an understanding of His Word.

The Lord has great things in store for you! Here is His promise:

"I know the thoughts that I think toward you," says the Lord, "thoughts of peace and not of evil, to give you a future and a hope. Then you will call upon Me and go and pray to Me, and I will listen to you" (Jeremiah 29:11-12).

God bless you!

YOUR NEW IDENTITY IN CHRIST

IF YOU HAVE PRAYED to surrender your life to Christ as your Lord and Savior, God's Word declares many incredible truths about your new identity. No matter what you may have done before being born again in Christ, in Him you are a *"new creation,"* and Scripture says, *"Old things have passed away; behold, all things have become new"* (2 Corinthians 5:17).

Take time to look up and meditate on these amazing verses about your new identity in Christ (1 Timothy 4:15). By faith, agree with what God's Word says about you, and claim His promises to you as His beloved child!

In Christ, you are…

- Justified, forgiven, and redeemed – Romans 3:24; Ephesians 1:7

- Crucified to your old, sinful self and raised to a new life – Romans 6:6; Ephesians 2:5; Colossians 3:1

- Free from condemnation – Romans 8:1

- Free from the law of sin and death – Romans 8:2

- Accepted by God – Ephesians 1:6

- Sanctified, holy, and set apart for God's purposes – 1 Corinthians 16:2

- Filled with wisdom, righteousness, sanctification, and redemption – 1 Corinthians 1:30

- Led in constant triumph – 2 Corinthians 2:14

- Liberated – Galatians 5:1

- Joined with other Believers in God's family – Ephesians 2:11-22

- An heir of God – Galatians 4:7; Ephesians 1:11

- Blessed with every spiritual blessing – Ephesians 1:3

- Chosen, holy, and blameless before God – Ephesians 1:4

- Sealed with the Holy Spirit – Ephesians 1:13

- Seated in a Heavenly position – Ephesians 2:6

- God's workmanship, created for a life that bears good fruit – Ephesians 2:10; John 15:5

- Near to God – Ephesians 2:13

- A partaker of God's promises – Ephesians 3:6

- Bold and confident in approaching God – Ephesians 3:12

- Transferred from spiritual darkness into God's light – Ephesians 5:8

- A member of the Body of Christ – Ephesians 5:30

- Hidden with Christ in God – Colossians 3:3

- Guarded in your heart and mind by God's peace
  – Philippians 4:7

- Perfectly provided for, with all your needs supplied
  – Philippians 4:19

- Complete – Colossians 2:10

As you meditate on what God says about you in His Word, you will be *"transformed by the renewing of your mind"* (Romans 12:2). Satan's lies and accusations about you will be replaced by your new identity as *"the righteousness of God"* in Christ (2 Corinthians 5:21).

Remember God's great promise to those who meditate on His Word and receive it as true in their lives:

> *Blessed is the man who walks not in the counsel of the ungodly, nor stands in the path of sinners, nor sits in the seat of the scornful; but his delight is in the law of the Lord, and in His law he meditates day and night.*

> *He shall be like a tree planted by the rivers of water, that brings forth its fruit in its season, whose leaf also shall not wither; and whatever he does shall prosper* (Psalm 1:1-3).

"Inspiration partners experience miracles in their circumstances as we join our faith to theirs and invite God to take charge of their situation."

- MARILYN,
  PRAYER MINISTER